when you're about to go
off the deep end,
don't take your kids with you

mykinashaw.co (Julia) (test)

"Kelly is the 'Dr. Phil of Parenting!' The book
spoke directly to my heart. The "Daring Do Over" idea
in *Chapter Nine* supports the behaviors I want in my
family and provides a powerful lesson in humility."
– Dianna Podmoroff "ULTIMATE MOM" OF JAYDEN 3 & TYE 1

Julie!
may your "deep ends"
be shallow & your
"shallow ends"
everlasting,
fondly
Kelly

publications available from

STEPPING STONES FOR LIFE LTD.

by Kelly E. Nault

CD

How to Raise Fabulous Kids in 10 Minutes a Day:
for Mom's with Little or No Time

BOOK

When You're About to go Off the Deep End,
Don't Take Your Kids with You*

PROGRAM

Ultimate Mom Self-Study Program

visit **www.ultimateparenting.com** for more details
or refer to the order information at the back of this book

*10% of the gross total proceeds of this book will be donated
to the Make A Wish Foundation—a charity that grants wishes of children
with life-threatening medical conditions in order to enrich
the human experience with hope, strength and joy!

when you're about to go
off the deep end,
don't take your kids with you

A Step-By-Step Guide to Permanently Eliminate
Chaos and Frustration in Your Home,
and Unleash the "Ultimate Mom" Within You

by kelly e. nault

STEPPING
STONES
for Life Ltd.

Wyoming, USA • Vancouver, Canada

Stepping Stones for Life Ltd.
P.O. Box 33019
1583 Marine Dr.
West Vancouver, BC V7V 1H0 Canada
1-888-233-5652

Or contact the author at: **www.ultimateparenting.com**

ISBN: 0-9734938-0-1

Author: Kelly E. Nault
Editors: Diana Podmoroff, C.S. Howe and Ernest Neumann
Illustrator: A1 Future Technologies
Original Design Concept: Designer Jeremy Kranz
Additional Design and Production: Sabre Design & Publishing
Final Production: basic elements design
Author's Photographer: Victoria Chan

**10% of the gross total proceeds of this book will be donated
to the Make A Wish Foundation**

First Edition 2004
Printed and bound in Canada by Friesens
♲ 100% POST-CONSUMER RECYCLED PAPER

loving dedication

To my Grandmother—my angel with silver hair
who taught me that berry picking, a long walk,
and a good chat over a cup of tea
can cure just about anything.

table of contents

table of contents

acknowledgements

Just as it takes a community to raise a child well, it was a community of people who helped me to successfully create *When You're About to go Off the Deep End, Don't Take Your Kids with You*. I thank them for lending a listening ear when I was about to go off the deep end. I am especially grateful to them for helping me celebrate when I managed to get myself out! It is with great pleasure that I honor each of them here, as I am a far better woman today for having them in my life. So here they are: the shining stars, the "gems of friends," and those who love me even when I'm stressed.

Michelle Anderson—Our weekly adventures have saved me years of therapy!

Elizabeth Atmore—For modeling what an "Ultimate Mom" can do.

Dr. Oscar Christensen—Your ability to motivate children, rebellious teenagers, and struggling parents taught me more than any graduate book!

Amy Dauphinee—Our laughter was often all I ever needed to keep on going.

Elvis—Your unconditional canine love is cherished!

Gloria Freeborn—Your courage to give me feedback made all the difference: Telling me what you loved, what you liked, and especially what you didn't.

Grant Hardy—Your words, actions and hugs have encouraged me so.

Graham Hardy—Our sushi parties and dinner dates are treasured times.

Trudy Hardy—Thank you for the gift of being part of an extended family.

Lori-Ann & Lawrence Keenan—Your generosity feeds my tummy and my soul.

Tom Matzen—Who inspires me with his brilliance, encourages me to be more than I already am, and loves me more than what I once thought possible.

Dr. Gary McKay—The impact you have had on the parenting world has motivated me to do the same.

Edna Nash—You are the "Queen of Encouragement!"

Dennis Nault—For being my "Ultimate Dad;" believing in me and loving me always.

Dr. Jane Nelsen—The authenticity in your best-selling books has influenced me deeply.

Kathy Verrelli—For being the first Mom to read this book, for motivating me with your emails, and cheering me on in the moments I wasn't so sure.

To You, The Reader—For demonstrating your commitment to being the best Mother you can possibly be, for picking up this book, and taking action!

There was also a fabulous team of Moms who reviewed the book, friends who said, "keep going," and colleagues and experts who contributed their wisdom! These wonderful people include: Dr. Bob Armstrong, Sheila Boyce, Meredith Deasley, Robin Elliot, Leanne Ewen, Naomi Fenson, Janice Golub, Susan Gottschick, Stefanie Hartman, Dr. Clair Hawes, Ross Hetherington, Caille Howe, Moya Jack, Cyndi Jacob, Jan Janzen, Suzanne Kyra, Paul and Leslie Lemberg, Erin Little, Ivy Milian, Dianne Orsorno, Heather Piechnik, Jenni Weston, and Joyce Wilson.

why you will want to read this book...

If you picked up this book, then you likely agree that raising children can be an all around hair-raising experience. It is, without a doubt, the most difficult job on earth! Fortunately, it can also be one of the most rewarding. Otherwise, what woman in her right mind would clamor to apply for a job with the following description?

WANTED

Woman Who Can Get by on Little Sleep for Long-term Position!
Seeking Female for Fulltime 24/7 Motherhood Position
(no education, no resume required).*

NO SALARY!

Responsible for nurturing, guiding, disciplining, housing, feeding, grooming, clothing and chauffeuring a human being for the entirety of its' childhood and adolescence. Few holidays. Expect interruptions during beauty sleep and coffee breaks. Organization an asset (but not necessary!). Ability to deal with whining an asset (but not necessary!). Prior experience with children an asset (but not necessary!).

NO PAY
(but you are responsible for covering all the child's needs and expenses!)

NO DENTAL COVERAGE
(be prepared to break the bank on braces for this human being!)

NO MEDICAL COVERAGE
(start putting money aside now!)

Job security guaranteed for at least 16 years
and can run as long as 75 years!

*NOTE: APPLICATION CAN TAKE UP TO NINE MONTHS TO PROCESS.

With job criteria like this, it's no wonder mothers don't go off the deep end more! At first glance, it would appear that no woman in her right mind would accept this position. Yet motherhood is not about the mind—it's all about the heart. This book brings to light the "heart" benefits of the "Mom-ming" role and helps make the journey more inspiring, rewarding, and enjoyable. Taking the time to read this book could be one of the best investments you will ever make—for both you and your children. This book shows you how to achieve the inner hopes and dreams you have for them little by little, day by day.

By the time you finish this book, I guarantee you will know how to create a home based on compassion, mutual respect, and open communication. These characteristics alone can prevent much of the needless pain that many families suffer because they just didn't know how to do it better. Reading this book also gives you the opportunity to prevent your children from feeling like they don't belong, like they don't have a "voice" and like they don't have freedom. Why is this so crucial? When children feel stifled (even by mothers who have the best intentions) they are more likely to make poor choices; ones that can take a mother's stress level through the roof!

These choices don't just affect us as mothers; there is an enormous price we pay as a community for raising children who lack true self-esteem. Many kids today are seeking a sense of belonging, power, and acceptance in all the wrong places—in gangs, in alcohol, in sex, in drugs and even in suicide. The discontent we see on the news, hear on the radio, and witness in our children's schools is our call to action.

I wrote this book in response to my concerns. Today, as a counselor, I see more and more frustrated, unhappy, and completely exhausted Moms dealing with children who are looking for what they can "get" out of life rather than what they can "give." Our world of instant gratification is churning out thousands of pampered children who are, in turn, becoming a generation of young adults who believe that they are entitled to handouts. When they are shocked to find that the "real world" requires more than what they believe they are capable of, they are left with deep dissatisfaction in their hearts, minds, and souls.

Yet, there is another way—a path that empowers children to shine brightly! Right now, you have the opportunity to learn a proactive parenting approach that utilizes the finest resource we have—our kids themselves! The practical information in this book will give you simple and effective strategies that can save you tons of time, frustration, and grief while having fun! No matter what your child's age, it is never too early or too late [*well, OK, if they are already in their 70's it may be just a bit too late!*] to lay the groundwork for your future together. As you read, you will find that the key is not just in this book, but in accessing what you have had all along—that incredible "Ultimate Mom" within you. **The "Ultimate Mom" training outlined in this book does not require that you add more to your "to-do" list, or get by on less sleep—the one requirement is that you become more of who you are by creating a life worth living with less stress and more joy!**

Shall we begin?

foreword by Dr. Gary McKay—

This book has something very special in store for you and your children. *When You're About to go Off the Deep End, Don't Take Your Kids with You* can be the bridge between the life you live now, and the life you dream of. In an upbeat fashion, Kelly Nault presents you with solutions to overcome obstacles that prevent you from creating your best family.

For the past 33 years, I have dedicated my books, my work, and my life to supporting parents in raising cooperative and respectful families. This journey has given me the opportunity to work with the best of the best in the parenting field. I am pleased to say that millions have used my work from *Systematic Training for Effective Parenting* (known as STEP), *How You Feel is Up to You,* and my latest book, *Raising Respectful Kids in a Rude World,* but there is still more to do. The world we live in requires we do so for the sake of our future generations.

Every so often someone comes along with a solution that can take our society to higher plateaus—Kelly Nault is one of these exceptional people who offers real hope. It is my deep honor to write this foreword for my student, friend and now colleague, Kelly Nault. I am pleased to share the parenting education torch with her. I have tremendous respect for her and her mission: to unleash at least one million "Ultimate Moms." I hope you take the opportunity to become one of them by deciding and committing to use these tools within your own family.

Kelly is a rare individual whose zest for life is contagious. She has a heart of gold and anyone who has the pleasure of meeting her feels it immediately. **Kelly's commitment to charity and giving 10% of the gross book proceeds to "Make A Wish Foundation"—a charity whose mission is to grant terminally ill children their dreams—is something to be admired.** Kelly walks her talk, lives her dreams, and inspires you to do the same. It's as if you get a boost of her enthusiasm as she guides you through every single word and chapter. Kelly has collected the wisdom of parenting experts before her and has effectively combined this with her own experience to create a ground breaking book that can save you years of stress, hassle, and frustration.

It is a book with impact that goes beyond what most parenting books cover: how to consciously design your life, how to effectively deal with money, and how you can best nurture yourself in order to give even more to your kids. As you begin the book you will read Kelly's heart-warming story about the amazing parental situation she encountered with two blind boys. This book shares the strategies that enabled her to influence kids she is proud of, and inspires you to do the same. If you are at a crossroads in your family life or believe your family could improve in some way, this book will enable you to make the 180-degree shift that can positively change the course of your life forever. Using the tools in this book can help you to create a more purposeful life, eliminate the hassles that are dragging you down, and gain the skills you need to successfully deal with conflict.

This is a book for you—for today and tomorrow. The two prerequi-sites are a belief in the possibility that you can inspire improvements in your family and the ability to take action. Start reading the program and let the magic unfold. I invite you to read, enjoy the benefits, and keep in touch with Kelly by going to **www.ultimateparent ing.com, where experts like me will share our practical parenting tips. I believe Moms around the world will see and hear a lot more from Kelly, and for this I am grateful.**

I now present you with Kelly's story—a story that can't help but transform yours.

Dr. Gary McKay
Psychologist and best-selling parenting author

IF BEING A MOM IS SO EASY, THEN HOW COME I WANT TO QUIT?

Many Thought We Wouldn't Succeed, but We Proved Them Wrong!

This is the very book I wish someone had given me when I was in the "deep end" with two kids who were driving me crazy! It is my delight to share these tools with you now. Even though this book was inspired by my journey, it is really about your own journey. I use my story and my client's stories as models for what you can do—for what any Mom can do! Before we begin, let me tell you a few things about myself, so you'll know how I became so passionate about, and committed to helping unleash the "Ultimate Mom" within Moms just like you!

What you might not know about me is that I am a parenting expert, who has never been married and has never had kids! Yet Moms, even dads, ask me for advice and they keep coming back for more! Why do I have anything of value to teach you? I don't teach you what has and has not worked for me with my own kids but I do share with you what has worked consistently for hundreds of my clients who are mothers. In addition to having a Master's in Counseling Psychology [*in which I spent thousands of hours learning what motivates children*], I have worked with children and their families for over ten years. Over the years, I have had the delight of facilitating parenting workshops in which I witnessed how proactive parenting tools (like those shared in this book) have transformed the lives of moms, step-moms, dads, step-dads, and even grandparents! When the tools are applied, happier parents and happier children are the result. But there's even more! I have also had the challenge and the pleasure of working with many of the "extreme cases"—the children that others have given up on.

My most difficult "extreme case" walked into my life just seven years ago. It was at this time that I was thrown into the "deep end" when I became a "caregiver" to two blind brothers. Graham was a serious seven-year-old and Grant was an imaginative six-year-old. My schedule consisted of approximately ten, 24-hour shifts each month, and I thought the job would be a cinch! I just had to be "Mom" while their Mom, an intensive care nurse, was working. When I accepted the job, I had no idea that the boys' behavior would soon have me vowing to never have children of my own.

Although our relationship started off well, their Mom warned me that the "honeymoon period" I was experiencing could end. It abruptly did—like a slap in the face! Suddenly, I encountered Academy Award winning temper tantrums, devious revenge tactics, and heated power struggles. There were many times that I seriously wondered if they would both end up in a juvenile delinquent center and I in some psych ward!

When I accepted the job, I didn't realize the extent of the boys' history of extreme misbehavior. If I hadn't experienced some of it myself, I probably wouldn't have believed it to be true. Their prior mischief, I found out months later, included intentionally peeing on a caregiver's bed, regularly banging on the walls, and attacking a caregiver while traveling on the public transit system. In the attack, the boys used their canes and teeth as weapons, leaving the caregiver with bad bruises and visible teeth gouges up and down the inside of her legs. It was their Mom who received the very difficult call. When she arrived home, she found an extremely shaken caregiver who refused to even step inside the house with the two boys. She left, never to return, leaving the boys' single Mom to take stress leave and figure out how to deal with her two out-of-control children.

When I heard these stories I became convinced that what they needed most was more discipline. If they were going to play hardball, I could play too; and I was determined to win! I was the adult in this situation, and I certainly wasn't going to let two boys get away with such disobedience. Surprise, surprise! It didn't get any better, it got worse! I realized I was losing the battle big time, the night Graham threw a plate past my head after I told him that there would be no stories because he refused to clear the table *[luckily, he is blind and has terrible aim!]*. Frustration, anger, and disappointment set in. How could I be doing everything right while they continued to do everything wrong? Parents, friends, and acquaintances suggested I quit—in fact, they thought I was crazy to continue. I cried, I wanted to leave, but I stayed. Why? Because I knew that somehow there had to be a better way.

Like a detective on a mission, I did everything in my power to find the missing key that would give me the "child raising nirvana" I desired. Fortunately, the solution wasn't far away. Because I had always been interested in families, I began my Master's in Counseling Psychology at the Adlerian School of Professional Psychology and was learning a new approach to child discipline. Soon it became obvious that *they* weren't the problem: I was! I had fallen into using the common, but ineffective, strategies of taking away privileges, using "time-outs," and nagging; believing that those punishments would actually motivate them to do what I wanted. I realized *[gulp!]* that I was helping to support the very behavior that was driving me crazy!

How You Can Save Years of Frustration from My Story Alone

Three years into my relationship with the boys, Graham said to me while riding in the car: "You know, since you have come into our lives I have learned a lot."

"Really?" I asked. "Yeah, I've learned things like vegetarian food can actually taste good." "Yeah!" Grant enthusiastically piped up, "And I don't misbehave nearly as much as I used to." "Funny," I thought, "Because I don't misbehave as much as I used to either."

I, like so many parents, used an ineffective approach that disrespected the kids and encouraged them to disrespect me. Why? Because I didn't know any better. Do you?

In your hands, you hold a book that covers every tool I used to transform the misbehaviors that made me want to jump off the deep end. It was out of pure desperation that I learned how to "go off the deep end" *without* taking the kids with me. **What I learned is a "feel good" method of parenting that naturally leads you to access the "Ultimate Mom" within you, so you will naturally nurture the "Ultimate Child" within them.** This new approach permanently eliminated the chaos and frustration I experienced on a regular basis. And aside from delivering great results, it has also proven to be a lot more fun. The foundation of what I share in this book comes from Adlerian psychology and has been time-tested, child-proofed, and designed for your greatest success as a Mom.

Why Adlerian Psychology?

To date, Adlerian psychology is the only philosophy I have found which consistently works to inspire positive behavior in any child! I looked long and hard to find such a solution. In my undergraduate degree at university, I searched for the answers to common family breakdown, frustration, and upset. But I never found them. I was disappointed to find a department of Professors of Psychology who were highly educated, highly published and yet, they themselves were going to marital therapy on an ongoing basis, were getting divorced like it was going out of style, and were taking their children to child psychologists because they were out of control. Something was terribly wrong.

Fortunately, one of my Doctoral instructors shared with me that if she were to begin her education again she would choose the Adler School of Professional Psychology. Who was Dr. Alfred Adler? I had no idea. I soon discovered that he was a contemporary of Freud and Jung but was largely unknown. Adler's theories present a cognitive and optimistic approach to what makes relationships work. His commonsense psychology, which has made a difference to millions around the world, was the first theory that made sense to me and delivered the results I was looking for.

In the three years of my graduate work at the Adler School, I had the pleasure of learning, modeling and being supervised by some of the world's greatest parenting experts including: Dr. Gary McKay, Dr. Harold Mosak, Dr. Clair Hawes, Edna Nash, and Dr. Oscar Christensen. Using their teachings as a base, I was not only able to get through the tough times, but began to experience less stress and much more joy. Suddenly, I was getting the respect, cooperation, and harmony that I had been seeking from the boys for over a year! I actually had the ideal parenting practice experience. After trying something new for a couple of days, I had the luxury of going home to regroup, recharge, and reevaluate. When I was stuck, I had the experts at my disposal. Knowing just how invaluable this was to me, **I have written this book for you and created a website www.ultimateparenting.com to support you in the very same way— giving you access to experts who deal in the real world, answers to your specific questions, and practical advice that can quickly have you on the path to a more fulfilling life.**

Wondering where Dad is?

Thus far, I have spoken much about you—about Mom! I have written this entire book specifically for you. In fact, I have chosen a capital "M" each time the word "Mom" is used to emphasize just how important you are! Yet, when it comes to parenting, "Mom" is not the only word. There are the dads—the stay-at-home dads, distant dads, roughhousing dads, devoted dads, and missing dads. So what about dad? If you are wondering where dad fits into all of this parenting stuff or whether we should just leave him in front of the TV watching football, allow me to answer. **Dads are very important!** By all means share with him when you are motivated to do so *[keeping in mind that pinning him down in order to stuff information down his throat is never the way to truly inspire him!]*. This book was specifically written to support you! If your family is blessed enough to have a dad who is a real keener, encourage him to read *Chapter Two* titled, *How a Mom Like You, Can Find Guilt-Free TLC,* in order that he may find ways of supporting you. **Dads who are seeking more effective ways to parent are also welcome to visit our site www.ultimateparenting.com in order to gain access to an abundance of parenting resources, which provide real results and solutions.**

How to Best Use this Book

Despite the seven years with the boys, a decade of working with children, and my Master's in counseling psychology, I caution you to not just take my word for it. **You are the expert in your life**. Your own common sense and intuition will direct you to know what is right for you and your family.

Before each chapter, you will find my diary entry that describes my own frustrations and joys of dealing with the boys, or success stories that I collected from mothers who have used the techniques I prescribe. The content within each chapter offers practical tools for getting results and concludes with a "Taking Action" Section that encourages you to use what you have learned for immediate benefit. Have little time? Just read the "Chapter Tips" toward the end of each chapter to get a sense of whether or not the chapter is worth your time. And if you are a freedom lover like me *[following the rules only when they make sense to you!]*, read this book in whichever way works best for you. Skip around, read it backwards, or be so bold as to go right to the end! I dare you. ☺

If you have a current problem you would like to fix, I have a solution. At the end of the book, you will find an index that highlights the page numbers where you can find answers to specific challenges you may be facing right now. The final chapter also invites you to join the *1,000,000 Ultimate Mom Challenge* at **www.ultimateparenting.com. The content within this entire book is**

essential and yet parts of it will be more applicable at certain phases of your and your children's lives. Keep it close by, as a reference, because you might never know when you'll be about to go off the deep end.

What I Wish for You, Your Kids, and Our World

In conclusion, I want to share with you one of the principles I strive to live by: to leave the world better than I found it. Together we have the opportunity to do just this. By gifting our future with kids who are skilled in conflict resolution, have the ability to form intimate relationships, and have the passion to contribute to our communities; we will naturally leave the world better than we found it.

What I wish for you... is the courage to risk experimenting with the tools shared within this book—tools that can transform your entire family's life today, tomorrow, and into the future. I wish for you the strength to follow your own wisdom, bountiful friendships that bring out your very best, and opportunities that require you to grow into a more beautiful and confident woman.

What I wish for our children... is a home in which their passions are nurtured, their opinions are respected, and their gifts are celebrated. I wish for them "Ultimate Moms and dads" who know how to help them actively pursue their dreams, how to lead them to recognize their own greatness, and how to inspire them to lend a helping hand.

What I wish for our world... is a future generation of adults who are capable of handling conflict with understanding, compassion, and skill: a generation of responsible citizens who consciously prepare to leave the world in a better way than they found it.

Dear Diary,

Today, I was determined to stay cool, maintain my sanity, and keep control! Yet, I now find myself doubting everything I am doing and am close to going off the deep end.

This morning I was having a pleasant dream about dancing in the exotic Congo. But then I awoke to realize that the drumming I heard was Grant banging on his walls. I glanced over at the clock which glowed 4:36 am! 'What the heck is he doing?' I wondered. I stormed into his room and told him to reserve his drumming session for an appreciative audience and then stumbled to the bathroom door, only to find that it was mysteriously locked. Surprise! Graham had decided to see if I could figure out the secret to unlocking it. At breakfast, sitting around a table that was surrounded by more Cheerios than ever reached a mouth, the bickering started. By eight o'clock the boys had lost their computer time for the week and all I kept thinking was, 'Just half an hour until I can drop them off at school and be free.'

When we finally got to Grant's grade one classroom door, two children had left knap-sacks to hold their place in line. I guided Grant to the back, third from the front, and said a quick good-bye before running for freedom. While sprinting to the car, I took one last parting glance over my shoulder to see Grant hurl the two knap-sacks into the air (almost taking out a student in the process!) and then, with a huge smile, use his white cane to victoriously sidle into first place. To say I was embarrassed would be an understatement! What am I doing here?
I just want my old life back.

Kelly

COULD YOUR APPROACH TO MOTHERHOOD BE GIVING YOU GRIEF?

How Can You Find Your Best You?

From day one of motherhood, there is some grief (sometimes a whole lot of it, depending upon the difficulty of labor!) Yet, becoming a Mother can also provide an extraordinary opportunity to find the best within you. There is a beautiful story that speaks of the beauty that lies within each of us. This is my version:

> A little boy passes a sculptor in an Italian square each day on his way to school. Seeing the sculptor painstakingly chisel away at a huge block of marble was such a familiar scene that the boy hardly noticed him. Seven months passed, and one day the boy realized that the chiseling he was accustomed to hearing had stopped. Curious, he looked up to see the finished masterpiece: a sculpture of a magnificent goddess. Awed, he asked the sculptor, "How did you know she was in there?" The sculptor smiled and answered, "Why she was in there all along. All I did was remove the excess marble that was hiding her."

This chapter, and this book, is about chiseling away the excess marble—the behaviors, habits and triggers—that are concealing the best that lies within you.

1

Is the "Pendulum of Parenting" Adding Unnecessary Frustrations and Guilt to Your Life?

The "pendulum of parenting" is a common pattern that is one of the obstacles that may prevent you from accessing the "Ultimate Mom" within. When something flies out of your mouth that you wish you could take back, when you feel taken advantage of, or when you think your children don't appreciate all that you do, chances are you are stuck in the "pendulum of parenting." **What is this pendulum? It is the practice of swinging back and forth: from being too soft and then too hard when disciplining our kids.** Why even mention this pattern? Because it is what causes much of the needless guilt, stress, and frustration that many Moms deal with on a daily basis. Once you eliminate the pendulum, you will have taken a super-heroic leap toward accessing the "Ultimate Mom" within you. When you do this, you will have the confidence and peace you deserve. Sound like heaven? Read on...

What causes the "pendulum of parenting?" It is the direct result of using out-dated parenting strategies that are based upon earlier generations. Although times have changed, many Moms are unconsciously operating as if the world has not. Only a few decades ago, social norms were based upon inequality in which people commonly viewed others as unequal to themselves. The majority of the public accepted class distinctions based on race, socio-economics, and gender as a way of life. White was better than black, dad was "head" of the household, and children were to be "seen and not heard!"

Fortunately, our children rarely see these models of subservience. This can be both a blessing and a real problem. Even though we don't want to go back to the "good ol' days" *[when women couldn't even vote!]*, it would sometimes be easier if our kids just did what they were told. Face it, children today are deeply aware of their rights and freedoms and will voice their opinions without being asked. Visit a playground today and you are likely to hear some version of, "Oh, yeah! I'll get my Mom to sue you if you say that one more time." Despite this change however, some frustrated Moms are still attempting to use the old method of "do as I say because I say so." These Moms seek to maintain control by using a "heavy-handed" approach to parenting. Yet, other Moms have swung to the opposite extreme using a "light-handed" approach. These two types of Moms can be described as follows:

- **Heavy-handed Approach Used by the "Mussolina Mom"**— She is the dictator *[not as well known as "the" Mussolini but she does want her way!]*—the boss, and knows it. And frankly, she kind of likes it! This Mom establishes a home of strict boundaries with little flexibility and has a quick temper. Her raised voice can often be heard dictating what to do, how to do it, and when to do it. Yelling, grounding, and taking away privileges are the ways this Mom attempts to "make" her kids listen. Her downfall? Her children find ways of secretly doing what they want anyhow and desperately seek a sense of freedom—many times in dangerous situations. Ultimately, this Mom is defeated on the battlefield of her own home.

- **Light-handed Approach Used by the "Pillowy-Soft Mom"**— This Mom is sweet, nice and a true pushover. She wants peace at all costs and uses passive approaches to deal with conflict; often reasoning with her children only to later give in. She is generally softer spoken, gives many "chances" and does for her kids what her kids could do for themselves. Her home is all about flexibility with little or no boundaries. Is there a downfall? The children run the household, dictating to her what to do and use guilt and manipulation to get their way.

Which style are you more likely to use when pushed to the edge? If you are like most Moms you will vacillate between the two styles—being too hard or too soft—creating a "pendulum of parenting" resulting in disharmony, defiance, and disrespect. **Unfortunately, swinging between these two extremes is not as much fun as being Jane in a Tarzan movie swinging freely from tree to tree. When the pendulum is in full swing, it can wear a Mom thin.** This begins to happen when "Pillowy-Soft Mom" feels taken advantage of. Her resentment slowly builds until she abandons all "niceties" and transforms into the screaming "Mussolina Mom" yelling such things as, "Go to your room!" "That's it. No TV for a week!" or "I'll give you a reason to be sorry!" But, even "Mussolina" eventually feels remorse and guilt over her exploding temper; leading her to transform back into "Pillowy-Soft Mom." Now she desperately tries to make it up to her kids until, wham-o, they take advantage of her again. The pendulum keeps swinging, sending Mom from one side to the other. The vicious cycle of the "pendulum of parenting" is not only ineffective, but also exhausting for both mother and child.

But there is good news! The pattern is completely curable. By combining the positive traits of the two styles; the flexibility of "Pillowy-Soft Mom" and the boundaries of "Mussolina Mom"—*voilà*, you can access the "Ultimate Mom" who is described below:

- **"Ultimate Mom"**—This Mom shares her emotions in a healthy way and encourages her kids to do the same. She supports her children in their lives, but also has a life of her own! "Ultimate Mom" focuses on what her kids can learn from conflict and provides flexibility within clearly defined boundaries. She follows her word; commanding respect so that she only has to say things once. With gentle firmness she holds her children accountable for their actions, inspiring and instilling responsibility, confidence, and honesty. All the techniques described in this book will use this "Ultimate Mom" approach to parenting. The downside? It takes time to learn. But, if you're game to continue chiseling away at the old habits, so am I!

The Good, Bad, and Ugly of Yelling, Spanking, and Punishing

When we are in the "deep end"—at the end of our rope—we will often grasp at the first thing we think of to stop the behavior that is driving us mad. "Pillowy-Soft Mom" suddenly goes into hiding and

"Mussolina" reigns supreme! If you are a Mom who has ever yelled, spanked or punished your child, you can join the other millions of Moms out there who, from time to time, have turned into a raving "Mussolina" right before their kid's eyes. When this happens, have you ever experienced that wee bit of satisfaction that comes from feeling like you've "won"? Satisfying? Or is it? When you notice punishment improves your child's behavior, it may be easy to wonder if punishment is an effective choice. So what's the problem then?

What we sometimes fail to recognize are the long-term effects punishment has on our kids. This past fall, while on a beach in Santa Barbara, I met a guy who shared a childhood spanking story that I will never forget. When he found out I was writing a parenting book he proudly told me how his single Mom had done a great job of disciplining him. He also shared that spanking had helped him to listen to his Mother, do what he was told, and learn about right and wrong. But then he began to laugh as he said; "It also taught me how to use the wooden spoon on *her*." I went for the bait. "How did it do this?" I asked. One Christmas, when he was only four, his Mother was angry with herself for forgetting to water the tree. As she got down on her hands and knees to pick up the needles, her son snuck into the kitchen. He got the pasta spoon (that doubled as the spanking spoon), and boldly, took a big whack at her behind [*just like she had taught him!*] yelling, "Bad Mommy, Bad Mommy!" Her response? She spanked him.

It's a Simple Principle: What a Mom Sows, She Reaps

Call it human nature, or whatever you like, but there is a natural tendency to seek revenge when we believe we have been unjustly punished. Kids know how to push their parent's buttons and have a toy box full of ways to get back at us: the silent treatment, poor grades in school, sudden Alzheimer's when it comes to chores, temper tantrums and using the granddaddy of all revenge tactics—"I hate you!" Not only do kids resort to revenge when punished, but in true "monkey see, monkey do" fashion will attempt to use our approach to get their own way later on down the road. Eldest children are especially prone to pick up on a Mom's authoritative approach and will attempt to pull rank, be boss, and tell their siblings what to do. Where do they learn this? Yup! From that pretty woman looking back at you in the mirror.

Seeking revenge is common and doesn't escape even Moms. We all know this one. Your "significant other" does something you really don't like or didn't think was fair *[like buying a big screen TV without your consent; making a huge mess with the kids and leaving it for you to clean up; or inviting friends over for dinner when you wanted a quiet night!]*. When this happens you may seek to hurt back by using your own version of the silent treatment; going on a bit of a shopping spree; or even rolling over with a "not tonight" comment.

Before I go on, I'd like you to take a very deep breath, because what I am about to say may seem totally crazy. **Using punishment such as shame, blame or pain to make your child feel badly only leads to worse behavior.** Best-selling author and one of my mentors, Jane Nelsen says: **"Children do better when they feel better."** Most of us instinctively know this to be true even when we have been taught to accept the exact opposite. It is important for me to note that I am not advocating we all turn into "Pillowy-Soft Moms." Having your children "feel good" so they can "do good," does not mean that you let them get away with murder.

Wait! Your Grandmother and Mother Might Just be Right!

If punishment leads to more pain and worse behavior, perhaps we should let go of all traditional forms of parenting. But wait! We don't want to 'throw the baby out with the bath water.' Before we "poo-poo" all our grandmothers' ideas about parenting; there is one basic value that our grandparents grew up with that can foster self-confidence in our kids like nothing else. This is the value of "contribution."

There is tremendous power in having our kids feel like a valuable member of the family team. This critical part of parenting was first introduced to me in a story shared by one of my favorite counseling professors, Dr. Oscar Christensen. Oscar grew up in a farming community where children were expected, and relied upon, to contribute to the family and farm. It was common practice, for fathers to teach their children (boys and girls) to drive the tractor by the time they were 11 or 12. In those days, the tractor was often of greater value than the farm itself. "How many of you would trust your child with all your wealth?" he asked our graduate class when he finished sharing. Then, with a wink, he reflected upon how this one act boosted his and his peers confidence more than anything else.

In today's world, unless you live on a farm or in a developing nation, this show of confidence is rarely possible. We no longer need our kids to help out around the house for our survival. Today "convenience" is a way of life: instant soup, instant entertainment, and even instant teeth whitener.

Our instant world requires less physical labor and thus, most children today have few chores aside from school and homework. The life of luxury that many kids lead includes a lot of time spent "zoning out" in front of the TV and computer. This provides children a major disservice; the price they can pay is a lack of pride, confidence, and passion that only comes from meaningful contribution. By simply involving your kids in the running of the household [*covered extensively in Chapter Seven*], giving them greater responsibility, and asking them for their thoughts and opinions, you can easily foster a sense of contribution that improves your child's self-esteem and improves their motivation.

What Does Every Child on this Planet Want?

The notions of teamwork, contribution, and involvement directly address our children's needs. What are these needs? **Kids want to belong; they want to feel valued, they need to feel important to you.** They want to be a part of the team and you, Mom, may very well be the captain and cheerleader! Toddlers start off seeking to find a meaningful place within the family; school-aged kids seek a place within their circle of friends;

and young adults seek a place within the larger community. Why is belonging so important? When a child feels that they belong, they have the confidence to really show up, to contribute their unique gifts to the world, and to deal with whatever challenges life brings.

Showing up fully in life is something many of us are not especially skilled at. What if we fail? What if we fall flat on our face? And, what if it doesn't work out? **Belonging is the fuel that gives our kids the strength and courage to go after their dreams, even at the risk of failing. This feeling of belonging is pure freedom, true unconditional love, and the greatest gift you can give to your child.**

When we don't believe that "I belong and I am valued," we miss our own party! We don't show up! And when we don't show up, we don't truly live. Children who grow up in rigid households that have few choices and opportunities commonly experience a lack of belonging. They strive to please others and they fail to experience and express their passion. Pampered children also don't feel a true sense of belonging because they don't feel of true value to others. Growing up expecting others to do everything for them leads these kids to feel unfulfilled and, frankly, bored with life. The cure is belonging— guide your child to find their own unique gifts so they can share them with their community. Provide the opportunities to make a difference. We all want to make a difference. Pampered children simply do not know how.

Why Pampering is Dangerous to Your Child's Self-Esteem

"Pampering a child is just as bad as neglect? Impossible!" I thought, while in my first graduate psychology class in parenting. I was astounded, 'How could this be?' I mean, 'wouldn't it be far better to shower your child with toys than abandon or neglect them?' The answer was "no." According to the Adlerian approach to psychology, an individual's mental health is based on how much he or she genuinely contributes to others. It was an interesting philosophy but I admit, it took me a while to buy into the fact that pampering was as destructive as my professors claimed.

It took me ten years of working with families to finally conclude that the evidence against pampering was irrefutable. The most extreme example of the negative impact that pampering can have on an individual came when I was working with "Jasmine." Jasmine struggled in her relationship with her "little 34-year-old brother." As our sessions progressed I began referring to him as "Little Prince." "Little Prince" often used Jasmine's home as a free B&B opportunity. He would eat them out of house and home, leave his dirty clothes all around the house, and consistently bring back their car without gas. The longest he had ever held down a job was two months; he had no savings, no friends, and no ambitions. Upon hearing her description I correctly guessed that he had been a pampered child. He had one mother and five sisters who did everything for him. "Little Prince" wasn't even expected to walk on his own until the age of five, when he became too heavy for any of his "Moms" to carry. The sad result is a grown man who still expects the entire world to dote on him and when that doesn't happen, he resorts to childish outbursts and temper tantrums.

This "little prince" mentality is reaching epidemic proportions in adults who believe that their family, community, and government owes them something. These people lack the confidence and responsibility to create what they desire. If you implement what I share in this book you need not worry about your child joining the masses of children growing up believing that they are entitled to everything while doing nothing.

The Secret to Getting the Respect You Deserve

An important aspect of making sure your kids do not turn into spoiled "little princes and princesses" is to create an environment where you deserve and receive respect. This may seem like a completely foreign concept, but I assure you, you do not need to climb the highest mountain searching for a wise sage to uncover the "Ultimate Mom" who knows how to get the respect she deserves. **That "Ultimate Mom" already lives**

in your heart. You have likely caught glimpses of her in the moments you have given a glorious hug, marveled at your child's unexpected wise words, or managed to remain calm in times of significant stress. When your heart swells with love, your eyes glisten, and your mind is powerfully quiet; you've found her.

Allow me to take the word "respect" and break it down in order to give you some ideas about how you can coax the "Ultimate Mom" to come out and stay.

1. **R**espect Them—Model what you want to see by respecting your children and expecting respect in return [*how's that for a mouth full!*]. Kids will model what they see. Often, we don't recognize that our tone and approach is disrespectful of our kids. The easiest way to determine whether or not you are being respectful is to ask yourself: "Would I use this tone and say what I am saying to a friend or even to an acquaintance?" If the answer is "no," then it is time to change your tone.

2. **E**ncourage Them—Knowing how to truly encourage your child will do absolute wonders when it comes to their self-esteem. World-renowned Adlerian Psychiatrist, Rudolph Dreikurs, stated: **"Encouragement to a child is like water to a plant." Without encouragement a child's spirit may never fully shine.** The most effective words of encouragement are those that say, "I believe in you," "You are important," and "You have a lot to offer" [*covered in Chapter Eight*].

3. **S**upport Them—**Supporting our kids requires that we refrain from "I told you so" comments.** When we support our children fully, we give them the opportunity to learn from their own mistakes. We are there for them through both the tears and the laughter.

4. **P**ositive Attitude—While it may sound like a Pollyanna approach, the fact remains: it works! Having a positive attitude can do wonders for your day, your week, and your life. When we wake up with a spring in our step, our kids sense this and respond accordingly. **The easiest ways to remain positive are to do what you love, get enough sleep, and show gratitude for all that you already have.** By focusing on what is great in your life you attract even more "greatness!"

5. **E**ncourage You—Moms need encouragement too! **Surround yourself with "gems of friends," be your own best friend, and take the time to recharge.** These personal supports will indirectly help you to be respectful and patient of your kids so they will be respectful and patient of you.

6. **C**are Enough to Let Go—Allowing your kids the freedom to experience some things on their own is one of the most respectful things you can do. Letting go of unreasonable expectations, negative comments, and little things [*that really don't matter!*] that nag us is key to unleashing the "Ultimate Mom" within you.

7. **T**rain—Taking the time for training means showing your kids how to do things on their own. With a hectic schedule, it can seem easier to do the task for your kids rather than take the time to teach them how to do it for themselves. **Yet, training is what gives our children a chance to develop essential life skills, to gain self-confidence, and to ultimately feel respected!**

Implementing **R.E.S.P.E.C.T.** will encourage the "Ultimate Mom" in you to receive respect without yelling, nagging, or begging! **When both you and your children start to experience respect on a daily basis, the sky is the limit as this is the foundation of living life to the fullest.**

Why You Want Your Kids to Eventually Fire You from Your Current Job as Mom

When you successfully help your children to respect others, to belong, and to contribute they will eventually fire you from your current position in their life. The catch is—you want them to! Ouch! Did you feel that one? When your kids are the most important aspect in your life, just thinking about their independence can create that "empty-nest" feeling regardless of how old they are. I will always remember the pang of hurt that I felt when I walked in the door and the boys (then aged eight and nine), failed to greet me. No exuberant hugs, no pleading for special playtime—they were so totally engrossed in their computers they didn't even bother to come down from their rooms. Suddenly, I was no longer *nùmero uno*.

As with any relationship, your relationship with your kids will naturally go through different cycles and stages. In the toddler stage you are often their "hero." In the child phase you are their "CEO" who runs their social calendar. In their teens you become their "Advisor to the Board" and hope that your children consult you when making crucial decisions. When you suddenly find yourself no longer at the center of their universe, it means they are growing up. The upside is that they will have created a new position for you. Chances have it that the more you use the techniques described in this book, the closer you and your child will become during every stage. It is important to realize that at every stage they need you and even want you!

Chapter Tips:

1. More than anything, your children want to belong. By giving them opportunities to contribute to the family, you will give them what they really want while you will simultaneously boost their self-esteem!

2. Doing for your children what they can do for themselves, robs them of the opportunity to learn, grow, and ultimately shine!

3. By respecting your children you will guide them to have respect for you.

Taking Action:

1. The fact of the matter is you are already doing many "Mom" things well! Before learning anything new, it is important to identify the special strengths you already have by answering the following questions:

   i. What do I already do well as a Mom?

   _____

   _____

   ii. What would others say I do well as a parent? *[if you can't think of anything, ask your children!]*

   _____

   _____

   iii. What can I do today that will make a difference for my child?

   _____

   _____

2. You can exponentially increase your success by identifying compelling reasons for accessing the "Ultimate Mom" within you. Write down your top three reasons for wanting to do so:

I want to access the "Ultimate Mom" within me because:

i. _____

_____

ii. _____

_____

iii. _____

_____

3. To follow-through and accomplish a goal, it is important to make a promise to yourself that you will do whatever it takes to achieve success. Read the following "Ultimate Mom" Oath (or create your own), then make the promise in your heart and sign the document. **To download and print the full page Ultimate Mom Oath certificate go to www.ult imateparenting.com/bookdownloads.** Consider putting it in a place where it will constantly remind you of what your goal is and what you will do to reach it. Making this promise to your kids can be even more powerful so consider affirming your oath in front of them.

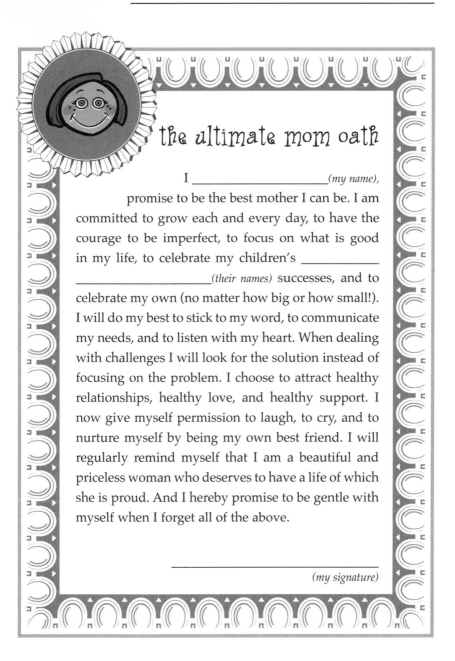

the ultimate mom oath

I _____(my name), promise to be the best mother I can be. I am committed to grow each and every day, to have the courage to be imperfect, to focus on what is good in my life, to celebrate my children's _____ _____(their names) successes, and to celebrate my own (no matter how big or how small!). I will do my best to stick to my word, to communicate my needs, and to listen with my heart. When dealing with challenges I will look for the solution instead of focusing on the problem. I choose to attract healthy relationships, healthy love, and healthy support. I now give myself permission to laugh, to cry, and to nurture myself by being my own best friend. I will regularly remind myself that I am a beautiful and priceless woman who deserves to have a life of which she is proud. And I hereby promise to be gentle with myself when I forget all of the above.

_____
(my signature)

Dear Diary,

It's 5 am and I am studying for my exam. The kid's lunches are not yet made, there are dirty dishes in the sink, I haven't answered email for a week and I desperately need to wash my hair. Maybe I could just use talcum powder instead? Graham needs help with the computer before school, Grant wants a story at breakfast and I've got an exam in two days!!! Yesterday, not only did I drop the kids off in my pajamas but I also picked them up in my flannels. I wasn't much fun to be around. I told the boys "my batteries are low," but I'm starting to believe that my batteries are not the rechargeable kind. How can I tell clients to work on their self-care, when I'm not walking my talk?

Kelly

Dear Diary,

Powerful is what I feel after telling my boss that I need to cut back my workweek. It took me months of worry and dozens of hours of discussions with girlfriends. But I did it. And, like I anticipated, she wasn't impressed. It was as if she believed that I was weak by saying that I am no longer willing to continue a "Super Woman" pace. But with this new schedule, I have found myself again.

And guess what? I actually like me! My clients like me and the kids love me! I had a fabulous morning walking to school with the boys; we made up tongue twisters, told stories, and even sang. Even though I am certain I messed up my chances of getting a permanent position, I don't care because my batteries are finally charged!

Kelly

HOW A MOM LIKE YOU, CAN FIND GUILT-FREE TLC

Five Reasons Why You do Not Want to Be a Mom Who Does it All

Thousands of Moms do it every single day. They ignore their own needs and strive to be, to do, and to make everything—you got it—perfect! But what isn't so perfect is the feeling of stress, burnout, and resentment that comes from trying to be a Mom who does it all. As Moms, we all know that a little self-care and some TLC (tender loving care) is what's "good" for us *[like broccoli]* and yet, most of us never get around to doing anything about it *[and Ben and Jerry's ice cream in the tummy sure tastes better than any vegetable!]*. So why is it so hard to do what is good for us? What Mom has the time! And isn't "sacrifice" the definition of what a good Mom is? Besides, our Moms did it, so why can't we? These are the very excuses that bring on the colds, the apathy, and the depression that prevents us from truly connecting with our kids, letting us see their gorgeousness, and being a Mom who is fun to be around.

Before you even consider skipping this chapter *[and some of you "Super Moms" will be tempted!]*, let me ask you this: are you perfectly happy with the speed at which your life is going? Do your kids really like hanging out with you? How about your friends, family members, or spouse—would they say that you are passionate about life? Do they see you enough to even know? If the answer is "no" to any of these questions keep on reading!

There are Five Reasons that You Absolutely Do Not Want to be a "Super Mom" Who Does it All

- **Lack of Balance = Lack of Fun**—When "Super Mom" turns into "Super Overwhelmed" she is not a pretty sight! Moms who are unbalanced fly off the handle, have less to give and thus, have less patience. "Super Moms" who stay up all night plowing through their never-ending "to-do" list wake up exhausted and grumpy day after day.

- **Poor Modeling**—For our sons, and especially for our daughters, "Super Moms" are the worst models when it comes to stress management. Moms who do it all model what it's like to be a rat in the rat race—spinning a wheel yet going nowhere fulfilled.

- **Greater Chance of Empty-Nest**—Moms who do it all, are more likely to experience depression when their kids leave home. Why? Because they are addicted to being needed and swooping in with their "Super Mom" cape to save the day. If your whole identity is "Super Mom," it can be devastating when your children grow up and no longer "need" you.

- **Danger of Pampering**—"Super Moms" tend to be the ones who do everything for their children because no one else does it well enough. Yet, when you do it all, you are robbing your kids and probably your significant other, of the chance to learn and to feel proud of what they can do for themselves.

- **A Life of Regrets**—"Super Moms" have more regrets in life because they do not take the time to just "be"—to stargaze, to bike ride, to watch a bee in the garden. They miss out on all those special, spontaneous moments with their children because they are forever thinking about the next task that needs to be completed. Later they regret what they missed out on or, worse yet, they push their children to fulfill their own unrealized dreams.

Why Failing to Ask For Help is the Most Selfish Act of All

Failing to ask for help is exactly what turns many "Super Moms" into "Super Overwhelmed." Are you better at giving than receiving? Here's a hint: if you are female, chances are good that you are! And if you are a Mom, well, this pretty much seals the deal. It should probably come as no surprise that women are the nurturers who give and give and give and give and give and give some more. Mother Theresa may be proud of us but our kids might be suffering because of it!

Here's the problem *[you knew this one was coming didn't you?]*: **when a mother's self-esteem becomes dependent upon "pleasing everyone else," when she gives out of obligation, and says "yes" before she thinks about how she is going to fit it in—she is headed for burnout.** As young girls, many of us bought into the belief that to mean something in this world we need to fulfill others' requests, to anticipate their needs, and to sacrifice everything we have at any price. The pitfall: in the process we sadly lose our vitality, our passion, and ourselves. Pleasing everyone is literally impossible. Like me, you may have spent a good part of your life attempting to do so. Am I right? But isn't it ever so *[sigh!]* tiresome and exhausting *[yawn!]*?

"But Kelly," you say, "It feels so good to please others!" **There is nothing wrong with giving; it only becomes a problem if you can't receive and when you give out of habit, rather than from the heart.** Some of us, myself included, have taken independence to such a level that our automatic response to, "Can I help you?" is "No." When we do not allow others to give to us, we are robbing them of the very experience we ourselves love to feel. We want to feel useful, helpful, and needed— Surprise! Your kids and your significant other want this too. So, have you been giving them the chance?

Could You Be Headed for Illness and Don't Even Know it?

When we don't let others give to us, we can actually be headed for illness without even knowing it. Our bodies are constantly giving us information—it's too hot, it's too cold. And those "gut hunches" that many call intuition are important indicators of what our needs are. Yet, "Super Moms" ignore these signals; which is just as dangerous as driving through a red light with your eyes closed or ignoring your car's warning indicators. When we ignore the small indicators they can turn into major warnings. If we ignore these major warnings we are headed for a major meltdown, complete exhaustion, or worse.

Fortunately, our bodies seek balance and keep us honest *[something has got to!]*. **Pain is our body's collect call to us—our choice is to accept the charges now, or pay greatly later on.** Being a slow learner in this area, I chose to pay later and pay I did!

Having been a "pleaser" at an early age, I pushed myself to excel in everything I did. I said "yes" to pretty much everyone's request, and failed to even acknowledge that I had needs. I then proudly ignored the warning signs: the exhaustion, anxiety, and dissatisfaction. Fortunately in college, I got a sickness called chronic fatigue syndrome, which resulted in sloth-like behavior. Sleeping for eighteen hours at a time was not out of the ordinary for me. Helpless, I found myself lying on the couch one day, realizing that I couldn't physically get up to make dinner. It was a call from my mother that led me to "rock bottom." After a bit of small talk she asked me how I was doing, "Fine." I lied, *[far be it for me to let anyone know that I might be doing less than fine.]* and then she asked, "Have you had dinner?" "No," I answered. Then she said, "Can you make dinner?" It was this question that pierced my soul, dissolved my mask, and brought tears to my eyes. "No," I whispered. The lie that I had lived for years was finally over and I knew it. Being this vulnerable was the key to my healing as it caused me to finally be honest with myself. The independent spirit and martyrdom I had adopted had failed me.

What about you? Are your days exhausting? Do you ignore your body? Are you too tired to be the woman that you want to be—that your kids want and need you to be?

Why Moms Need to Give Up Perfection

It may come as a complete shock to many Moms out there but no one, including you, is perfect. **It is our imperfections that actually make us human! When we do as Rudolph Dreikurs says, and "have the courage to be imperfect," life will become easier.** Embracing our imperfection gives us the opportunity to see all the awesome things about ourselves: to acknowledge the fact that we do have nice eyes, nice breasts, nice legs, nice whatever! And as we stop hiding our flaws, suddenly our psychological zits can become beauty marks!

I acknowledge it is not easy to do this. We are bombarded with perfect idealized models of what a woman should look like: sexy, 5'8", 125 lbs, flawless skin, legs and lashes that go on forever and ever, with airbrushed everything. But these ideals are unattainable *[even models will admit to looking better in photos than in reality!].* **It is sad that we believe we need to be someone other than who we are to be truly lovable. It is time to come clean with ourselves, for the gender of woman, and for our children by beginning to love the person we are, flaws and all.** I invite you to now stand and do one of the cheesiest things you may have ever done. Stand and say out loud, *"I am a gorgeous woman and am wonderful just as I am; now and forever. I am worthy, I am confident, I am lovable, and I _____(your name) am a Goddess!"* Yup, I mean it! Don't worry; no one needs to know but us. Go to the mirror right now, feet flat on the floor and say it. Then yell it out for your neighbors to hear! And remember to say it again and again, for the rest of your life.

How You Can Enjoy Guilt-Free Luxury

Moms tend not to treat themselves like the gorgeous women they are and when it comes to spending money they sometimes put themselves dead last. Many Moms restrict buying those small luxury items that say, "I matter!" Luxuries like flowers, bubble bath, and that cute little purse that becomes your favorite *[even when you may have many perfectly decent ones filling your closet!].* Treating yourself to a luxury now and again is not about money, it is about honoring the "Ultimate Mom" that is within you.

This chapter's "Taking Action" section will explain how to open your own "Ultimate Mom Luxury Account" so you can purchase those "special" indulgences guilt-free—a chocolate covered strawberry, a decadent massage, a little sparkly bracelet; anything that says, "I deserve to be treated too!"

How to Carve Out More "You Time" with Mom Time Management

Even if she wants to, what Mom has the time to treat herself? Once you have a little extra money and have begun the process of embracing your imperfections, you may have more incentive to find a time management strategy that works for you.

Eight Time Management Tips for Mom:

1. You don't have to check off every single item on your checklist to make it a successful day *[hallelujah sister!]* Just carry the items over to the next day.
2. Do that one hard task you have been putting off first—you can't imagine how cleaning that one item off your plate will motivate you to do even more.
3. Write your "to-do" list before you go to bed each night. Keep paper next to your bed so you can jot things down as you think of them instead of attempting to remember them all through a sleepless night.
4. Only put a maximum of six items on your "to-do" list each day. Prioritize and give yourself a realistic time frame to complete each item.
5. Each morning ask yourself, *"What one thing could I do to make this a truly spectacular day, and when am I going to do it?"*
6. It is better to do a little of something, than nothing at all. A ten-minute walk instead of an hour workout is far better than nothing at all.
7. Do your best to schedule for yourself at least one "play time" slot each week where you don't schedule anything at all!

8. Each week write down three special people in your life and think of one thing that would make a real difference to them. Remember to include "you" in that list—and often!

How to Become the World's Best Sleeper by "Draining Your Brain"

One of the biggest challenges with getting through our "to-do" lists is not having enough energy. Lack of sleep is something all Moms can identify with. Getting to bed is hard enough, but unfortunately all too many Moms find it hard to get to sleep even after they are lying down! If you are anything like me, lack of sleep can create a pretty grumpy Mom the next day. The key is to perform a "Brain Drain" before going to bed by dumping out your worries and inviting peace into your mind and heart. This can be done numerous ways including:

- **Journaling**—It doesn't take long to journal some of your thoughts, feelings, and concerns before going to sleep. Physically, writing out your thoughts creates the sense of having "dumped them."
- **Attitude of Gratitude**—Thinking or writing about what you are grateful for can lull you to sleep with a smile on your face.
- **Breathing Techniques**—There are many breathing techniques included in the next section. Relaxing in this way has the effect of "counting sheep."

How You Can Benefit from the Power of Your Breath

There are more kinds of breathing techniques than kinds of candy. The power of breath has been gaining popularity with the surge in meditation and yoga. We can go for weeks without food, a couple of days without water, and only a couple of minutes without a breath. Breathing techniques are one of the most useful "brain drains" I know. I have included three of the simplest here:

Three Simple Breathing Techniques:

1. **Noticing Breath**—Noticing your breath brings you into the present moment. When we are stressed, we often hold our breath. Unfortunately, this is also the worst thing we could do! The more we are aware that we're holding our breath under stress, the more we can change the behavior.

2. **The Full Circle Breath**—This is an excellent way to let go of a hectic day. Begin with a comfortable number of seconds—say three. Now breathe in from your belly for three seconds; hold your breath for three seconds, then exhale for three seconds and finally hold again for three seconds. This is one full cycle. Start off with three or more cycles and work your way up.

3. **Color Breath**—This technique is particularly helpful for those of you who are highly visual. Choose a word like peace, harmony, or vitality—any word that describes what you would like to experience. Then choose a color that represents this word. As you begin say, *"I choose to be/feel _____ (your word) and let go of anything that is not in my highest good."* As you slowly inhale imagine the air being tinted your chosen color. Visualize the breath going into your body, filling up your lungs and extending out to the rest of you. As you exhale imagine that you are letting go of anything that does not serve you. Continue until you have filled your entire body with this feeling.

How to Create "A Room of Mom's Own"

When you are doing things like breath work or other stress-busting techniques, it is helpful to have a quiet space. Sometimes the only quiet space in the house is the bathroom. Yet, with kids banging on the door or suddenly needing the use of the "throne," this isn't always the best place.

If I could give a gift to every woman in the world, it would be the luxury of having a room of her own—a place to let the tears flow, a place to seek solitude, a place to celebrate who she is, a space to be herself without any demands or interruptions like, "Hey Mommm!"

Imagine—a private space that is solely designed to replenish your energy and recharge your batteries after a long day. My secret dream has always been to own a luxury tree house—just a space of my own where even my kids wouldn't be allowed without an invitation. I would nap up there, nesting like a bird in a big ol' tree. For now, you and I might not have the space to have an entire room or tree house dedicated to ourselves but we can create a virtual room of our own by doing the following:

- **Journaling or Reading**—Journaling or reading in the morning for a mere 15 minutes can be a therapeutic experience—an "emotional retreat."
- **Crafting**—Some Moms are great with their hands and find therapy in expressing themselves through art. Whether it is knitting, scrap booking, or painting—get swept away by busying your hands and quieting your mind.
- **Treasuring**—Create a space where you can store your most precious treasures that make you smile. A drawer in the bedroom reserved for special mementos; a little altar of your favorite things on your dressing table; or even a treasure box where you store all your lovely keepsakes—your journal, favorite picture of yourself, love letters, favorite quotes, affirmations and prayers.

Mom's Own Stress-Busting Visualization

Aside from having a room of our own, we can use visualizations to reduce stress and provide TLC when we need it most. Visualization helps us to focus on what is most important: letting go of frustration, sharing greater love, and being completely present. Below, I have included a portion of the *Ultimate Mom Relaxation Visualization* that is the last track on my CD *How to Raise Fabulous Kids in 10 Minutes a Day: for Moms with Little or No Time*. Purchase this CD on our website **www.ultimateparenting.com/cd or use what I have included below to create your own.**

Find a quiet place where you can be completely comfortable. Take a deep breath in—deep down into your belly, exhaling through your mouth. Every time you breathe in, feel your breath fill you with energy; feeding you feelings of peace, harmony and tranquility. Say quietly to yourself, "I choose to focus all my energy on my heart to experience the joy I deserve while letting go of everything that does not support me."

Visualize yourself sitting in the most beautiful outdoor place you can imagine. This could be a real place you have visited, a place you want to visit, or one that you now create in your imagination. Smell the comforting smells, see the warm sights, and hear the calming sounds. Here you are completely safe. Here you are protected. Stay here for as long as you need to. Soak it all in.

Now look over in the distance and notice the dark rain clouds. You feel calm and safe watching them. As you look at them choose to surround yourself in a big nurturing bubble. Choose a color that you want the bubble to be. Sit quietly in your bubble feeling the protection and safety that it provides. As you sit in your bubble the storm clouds get closer and closer, but the closer they come to you the calmer you feel. Now the rain cloud is right over top of you. Each drop falls onto the outside of your bubble and gently slides off. Faster and harder it falls while the calmer and calmer you become. Finally, the cloud moves on and rolls off into the distance leaving only a quiet and beautiful sunshine day.

Again focus on your breath, feeling the confidence that comes with knowing that your bubble will protect you wherever you go today. Take another deep breath. **Know that you deserve to feel and experience love and peace even in the midst of chaos. Know that your boundaries will give you the ability to easily and effortlessly handle whatever comes.** Stay with the breath until you are ready to come back to your day with more energy than you felt before; feeling loved and feeling cherished.

How to Exercise Without Going to the Gym

Now that we have exercised our emotional body, it is important that we exercise our physical body. We all know that regular exercise reduces stress. Yet, with all your priorities, your weekly workouts may not make the cut. Use the following suggestions to give your physical body a boost. If you regularly workout *[Jane Fonda would be proud!]*, the suggestions below will give you ideas for those days when you miss a workout!

Six Ways to Exercise Without Going to the Gym:

1. Take the stairs whenever and wherever possible!
2. Instead of watching your kids play at the playground—play with them—swing on the swings, kick around a ball, and go down that slide!
3. Short walks are better than none at all! Get your kids involved by making walks fun with made-up stories, tongue twisters, and songs. How about walking to school?
4. When cleaning, become a "dancing queen!" This will make the time go faster and will also burn calories.
5. Get an exercise partner to help keep you committed.
6. Set an hourly alarm and do 10 jumping jacks, push-ups, and/ or crunches—a friendly reminder to exercise.

"Ultimate Moms" GET A LIFE—do You?

Exercise is just one aspect of giving yourself TLC. "Ultimate Moms," unlike the "Super Moms," know that the best way to give more to their kids is by getting TLC. Fully unleashing the "Ultimate Mom" within you means supporting your children to have a good life but it also means having a life for yourself. How do you know when you "have a life?" **When you regularly notice the preciousness in simple things (a sunset, your kid's toes, an older couple walking hand in hand), when you laugh from deep in your belly, and when you enjoy the journey of your life instead of focusing on the destination; then, you've "got a life!"**

Tall order? You see, this is the interesting part. Moms who live by this principle actually report having less stress, less items that they "have" to do, and less days of sadness because they are living a life that feeds them rather than depletes them. The best TLC you can give yourself is to create a life that you and your kids can be proud of. Why do we want to move towards this? Because Moms who do, make a difference in their very being. They are able to look back on their life with joy in their heart; knowing that they lived through the tears and through the laughter and have found a deeper appreciation of who they are, where they came from, and where they have yet to go.

Chapter Tips:

1. It is our imperfections that make us human. Moms who strive to be perfect, who attempt to do it all, and who only know how to say "yes" are headed for exhaustion, disappointment and regret down the road.

2. Asking for help from your children and loved ones is a gift to them!

3. When it comes to your "to-do" list, include at least one thing a day that is just for you and make it a priority!

Taking Action:

1. Choose a jar, box, or special wallet that you will call your **"Ultimate Mom Luxury Account."** The money that will be placed here is for the sole purpose of buying little luxuries for yourself. Where will this money come from? Anytime you consciously save money *[skip the coffee, find a meter that is paid, or quit smoking!]*, "deposit" this saved amount into your luxury account. Now here is the fun part! Once a month, spend whatever is in your account on a gift for you that will bring you joy. Only use the cash you have put aside, as these

purchases are to be entirely guilt-free!

2. Next time someone asks "Can I help you?" just say "Yes!" and then figure out how.

3. Start your day off right!

- **Choose to use an affirmation** like the one discussed in this chapter: *"I am a gorgeous woman and am wonderful just as I am; now and forever. I am worthy, I am confident, I am lovable, and I _____(your name) am a Goddess!"*

Or

- **Ask yourself:** *"If I did one thing today that would make this a truly spectacular day what would it be and when am I going to do it?"*

Or

- **Create a visualization audiotape or CD.** No time? **Purchase the "Ultimate Mom" relaxation that is included on my** *"How to Raise Fabulous Kids in 10 Minutes a Day"* **CD at www.ultimateparenting.com/cd.**

Dear Diary,

It was my sweet heart and my one month anniversary yesterday and it's as if we have been together an entire lifetime. From our first "business meeting" over lunch (which lasted five hours!), to the 11 hour phone call before our first date (when we discussed our grandchildren!), to the rediscovery of a list that took me from dream to dream man.

Only a year ago, I was struggling in a relationship that had lasted six years. I agonized over whether to stay. This motivated me to create a list detailing my dream relationship—it took me 10 minutes to jot down the 44 items, and even less time to forget about it. Little did I know, that I was creating my future.

Three days after meeting Tom, I pulled out my forgotten list. Glancing over the items, I quickly realized he had all but two of the qualities: "good cook" and "handy around the house." 'Well, no one's perfect,' I thought. Together, we went over the list [yes, a bonus—he didn't think I was crazy to have this list in the first place!] and when we got to "good cook," he jumped in with "Do you know that after I retire I want to go to cooking school to become a chef?" Then I got to "handy around the house." 'No, he couldn't be,' I thought. Again, he surprised me with, "I just renovated my condo—put in hardwood floors and new tiling." When we finished off the list Tom enthusiastically said, "Oh we're going to get married for sure!" It was astonishing. It was as if I had written that list to describe him in detail. I need to keep dreaming and dreaming well because, I really can get what I wish for!"

Kelly

"GET A LIFE!"
FOR THE SAKE
OF YOUR KIDS

Hold Onto Your Dreams—For You and Your Kids' Sake!

- What if fairies lived in your garden?
- What if a fairy godmother granted you three wishes?
- What if you felt deeply loved 24 hours a day?
- What if you could become whatever you wish?

The world of possibility, the "what if" mentality, is the world our children live in—the world from which we all came and the world to which we can all return. Although our kids start off in this "what if" world, by the time they enter school their spark for life is often hidden. But you Mom, can keep their flame burning. What's the best way to do this? Easy. Only when you ignite your own heart, dreams, and passions can you truly help your children to do the same. Every dream starts with that single first step and requires that we consciously choose to design our life rather than just let life happen.

Do You Know Where You are Going in Life?

If I called you up right now and said, "As a *When You're About to go Off the Deep End* reader I would like to take you out for dinner tonight and find out what you like about the book. Are you interested?" Excited, you reply, "Yes!" but as soon as you hang up you realize that I didn't tell you which restaurant or at what time. You don't even have my phone number or E-mail address. How easy would it be for you to find me tonight? Probably next to impossible! Knowing where it is that you are to meet me makes it much more probable that you will arrive.

It is the same with life. Knowing where you are going is crucial to getting there. And once you know where it is that you want to go, you can easily formulate your plan—your route. Having a plan does not mean your priorities become stagnant or that over time you won't encounter a few traffic jams, bumpy roads, or storms. **Having a clear direction in life simply increases the odds of you getting where you want to go.** So where do you want to go in life? Who do you want to be? Do you know?

How to Uncover Your Passions While Having Fun

Each of us has unique interests, skills, and passions. Sometimes these are concealed, but there is no time like the present to reveal them to yourself, to your kids, and to the world! Why do many of us have trouble identifying our passions? Because our parents and our schools did little to nurture them—instead we were encouraged to become "well rounded." Although being a "well rounded," Renaissance Woman may be useful; it is our passions that make life worth living.

Children naturally dream big—often in 3D color with surround sound! They also have a great knack for finding the extraordinary in the plain and ordinary. Uncovering your passions requires a similar approach; sometimes an ordinary skill or hobby that you take for granted can turn into something truly extraordinary.

How to Uncover Your Passions:

1. **Search through your old photo albums, schoolbooks, and journals.** As you leaf through ask yourself, "If I didn't know this was me which guesses would I make about what this girl loves to do? What does she enjoy most? What makes her heart sing?"

2. **Ask your trusted friends, family members, and colleagues to identify your strengths.** Sit down over lunch and review what they have written. Soak in the compliments!

3. **Write down your ideal day, month, and year.** Set the timer for half an hour and go to town writing. Afterwards, identify anything that you would like to incorporate now.

4. **If you had all the money you would ever need what would you be doing?** Answer the question: "What would I be doing now if I had enough money to live well?"

5. **Try new things.** New experiences can open up passions we didn't even know existed. Go through your community center's catalog and choose to take one new course you never considered before. Belly dancing, anyone?

6. **Notice your passions.** Begin to notice when your heart takes flight, when hours seem like minutes, and when you are in a special groove where time stands still. These will be the times when you will be living your passions and are doing what you love.

After going through the above exercises, look for patterns and identify what fills your heart the most. Then take it one step at a time. **Life was meant to be lived from your heart. Living from the heart naturally occurs when we do the things that best express who we are. When you do this, you will be showing up for life more fully, waking more energized, and wanting to give to others more spontaneously—simply because you have more to give.**

Create Your "Wish Upon a Star 100 List"

One way to supercharge your life is to create your "Wish Upon a Star 100 List." Do you remember the song, *When You Wish Upon a Star* from Disney's cartoon *Cinderella*? The first two sentences of the song are: "When you wish upon a star, makes no difference who you are, anything your heart desires will come to you," and "If your heart is in your dream, no request is too extreme." This song represents that "what if" realm of possibility that we spoke of earlier in this chapter and it gave me the inspiration to establish the "Wish Upon a Star 100 List" I share with you now.

This list is a physical record of all your wishes, desires, and dreams. My own personal list includes skills I want to learn, things I want to have, places I want to go, and things I want to experience. The dreams I have range considerably and include: swimming with dolphins, receiving my PhD, learning how to harmonize, going to a drive-in movie [how I ever missed doing this one I will never know!], and becoming a best-selling author. Anything goes when it comes to this list because as the song says, "No request is too extreme." The only criterion is, "Does it come from my heart?" If the answer is a resounding "Yes!" then write it down.

Why do I encourage you to create your own "Wish Upon a Star 100 List?" **Physically writing down your dreams is important because the things that get down on paper tend to get done.** The act of writing out your list also tells your subconscious that you are serious about your dreams. Your list is dynamic and fluid; it changes and grows with you over time. The items on your list are not written in stone and you are free to change them at will. A Mom who has more than one hundred dreams knows what she wants, has a deeper sense of purpose, and is more excited about her life. **And when Mom is happy, the kids will be happy too.** This alone makes the exercise worth doing!

Once you have completed your list I encourage you to review it from time to time and commit to checking one item off each year. Having started my own list over four years ago, I am proud to say that out of the original 144 items [being a bit of a keener I wrote down more than 100!] I have checked off 21 items which include: scuba diving at the Great Barrier Reef, standing in the Sistine Chapel in Rome, snowshoeing under a full moon, going on a silent retreat alone, doing my pre-doctoral at a local university, creating my own website, and accomplishing balance in my life more days than not. Inspired yet? What do you dream of? Jumping out of a plane? Skinny-dipping in a summer lake? Writing your life story? Making homemade truffles? Running for mayor? Donating one million dollars to charity each and every year? Going back to school? Being pulled by dog sled across the tundra? Now it's your turn!

Why You Need to Schedule Time for Passion

Are you starting to get a clearer picture of what you want in your own life? What we focus on can literally transform our life! **Our intentions and dreams are the seeds that produce the flowers of our tomorrows. Being clear about what we want ensures our "life garden" is filled with beautiful flowers rather than weeds that we don't even remember planting.** If your life is currently filled with a lot of weeds, it is time to consciously add the things that bring you passion rather than continuing to move unhappily through the motions of life.

Why is focusing on your passions important? Regularly including the things we enjoy in our life means having more joy to share with our kids. When you put off and ignore the things that bring joy, your heart suffers and you have less energy and love to share with your precious children.

If you are like most Moms you are a fabulous "multi-tasker." This skill can be used to your advantage when choosing to carve out time for your passions. Scheduling your own time (even 15 minutes a day), to include some of your passions is fundamental to unleashing the "Ultimate Mom" within you: create a scrapbook, tend your garden, read novels (that make your heart burst), journal your thoughts, or find a part-time job or volunteer position you love.

Just too busy? It is important to remember that the only clock ticking is your own. We are each given 24 hours a day. It is normal to have your priorities shift dramatically when you become a Mom. But I am here to tell you that life doesn't have to be an all-or-nothing proposition. Being Mom is only one role out of the many in your life. **If you fail to nurture** the other aspects of yourself including lover, artist, friend, sister, daughter, and dreamer you may end up driving down your life road on empty—going nowhere. Fill yourself up!

How to Use Affirmations to Jump-Start Your Best Life

When it comes to designing your own extraordinary life, affirmations are the mental power tools that build you a new life from the inside out. The beliefs we hold about ourselves are powerful. You are where you are because of the beliefs you hold. All the decisions you make are based upon what you believe about yourself, about others, and about how life "should be." For many of us, our core beliefs have not changed much since we left our parents' home. Some are useful, while others are not helpful in getting us to where we want to go. Which beliefs are helping you get to where you want to go? And which ones are not?

One of my favorite stories is about the old Cherokee Chief who is teaching his grandson about life.

> "A fight is going on inside me," said the grandson. "It is a terrible fight between two wolves. One is evil—he is anger, envy, sorrow, regret, greed, arrogance, self-pity, guilt, resentment, and ego. The other is good—he is joy, peace, love, kindness, empathy, generosity, truth, compassion, and faith."
>
> "This same fight," says the old Cherokee, "is going on inside you and inside every other person too."
>
> The grandson thought for a moment and then asked his Grandfather, "But which wolf will win?"
>
> The Old Cherokee simply replies, "The one you feed."

What you feed the mind is what will be true for you. Affirmations can help you feed the supportive wolf within you. They are declarations or statements that, in fact, starve the unhealthy beliefs and help you to establish new truths. Einstein recognized the power of the mind when he said, "Imagination is more important than fact." Thus, do not underestimate the power of affirmations, since although on the surface they can appear frivolous or foolish, they hold significant power.

There are as many affirmations as there are words in a dictionary, with endless patterns and purposes. The key to choosing an affirmation is to pick one that directly highlights what it is that you want to have in your life. When you are using affirmations make certain that they are stated in present tense rather than future tense. For example you would say, "**I attract** healthy support and nurturing friendships into my life easily and effortlessly," rather than "**I am going to** attract healthy support and nurturing friendships into my life easily and effortlessly."

The distinction between using affirmations stated in the future and present is crucial, as the mind does not know the difference between what is real and what is imagined. If you feed the mind an affirmation that is supposed to happen in the future, it will forever think of it as something coming in the future instead of attracting it to you *now*. These are the subtle, "sleight-of-hand" tricks you must employ when using an effective affirmation program. Choosing an affirmation is only the first step. **Affirmations become effective when you use, feel and believe them!**

How to Create Effective Affirmations:

1. **Use Them.** Most often I recommend using affirmations at the start and at the end of your day when the subconscious works its magic best. However, affirmations are portable and can be used throughout the day: waiting in the doctor's office or at a red light, while sitting in a boring meeting—anytime is a good time. Saying them in your head is useful, but it is even more powerful to say them out loud while writing them down.

2. **Feel Them.** This is the most essential ingredient for affirmation success. Without this your affirmation is pointless. If you are saying an affirmation like, "I am an 'Ultimate Mom' who deserves wealth," you don't want to be feeling like you are in a dentist's chair having a root canal. To generate authentic feelings use your imagination to act "as if" your affirmation were already true.

3. **Believe Them.** When you regularly repeat a positive affirmation that is in present tense (with the intention of using it for everyone's highest good) and say it with deep conviction, you will start to believe and then achieve. It is normal to feel skeptical. One of the best suggestions I have heard to overcome this feeling is from motivational speaker, Frederick Lehrman. He suggests affirming the following: "My affirmations work for me whether I believe they do or not."

Amazing Things Happen When You Use Affirmations

The first time I used affirmations I used them as a kind of dare. I wanted to find out whether they worked or didn't work, once and for all. I was applying for university scholarships, which in the past proved to be unsuccessful. It was a frustrating process when they didn't produce any money because each application required many hours of my time. After spending three hours on one particular scholarship, I received a notice telling me that graduate students were ineligible. [*I thought they would have included this in the guidelines!*]. I was discouraged.

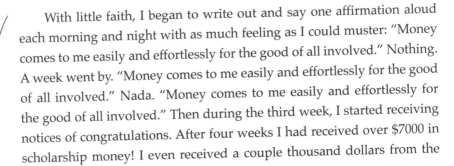

With little faith, I began to write out and say one affirmation aloud each morning and night with as much feeling as I could muster: "Money comes to me easily and effortlessly for the good of all involved." Nothing. A week went by. "Money comes to me easily and effortlessly for the good of all involved." Nada. "Money comes to me easily and effortlessly for the good of all involved." Then during the third week, I started receiving notices of congratulations. After four weeks I had received over $7000 in scholarship money! I even received a couple thousand dollars from the scholarship that had originally declined my application because I was a graduate student. They changed their mind! A person on the committee called me and told me that in his 16 years on the board he had never seen the committee change the rules. Coincidence? Well, whatever you want to call it, I was thrilled and $7000 richer. Intrigued? The only way to find out is to try it for yourself. Go on! If something spectacular just happens to occur let me know by contacting me at **www.ultimateparenting.com.**

Now that You Know What You Want, What Kind of Woman do You Want to Be?

So far this chapter has focused on what you want out of life. The real benefit of determining what it is you want is in the discovery of who you need to become in order to get what you want. Take some time now to think about your "Wish Upon a Star 100 List"—the things you want to have, how you want to contribute, and what you want to learn. Now ask yourself:

- Who would I become if I fulfilled every item on my list?
- How do I want my children as adults to describe me?
- How can I become an "Ultimate Mom" now?

The last question is the most important of the three. Focusing on the "Ultimate Mom" within you will enable you to support your dreams to start unfolding now.

The Key to Experiencing Greater Joy in Your Life Now

The key to experiencing greater joy is simple, but because it requires taking responsibility for our life, we often ignore it. Why? **It is easier to blame someone else when our life is not working rather than step up to the plate and do something about it. Life is not what happens to us; life is what we *do* with what happens to us.** Out of tragedy, abuse, and apathy women all over the planet have risen to experience joy—now it is your turn!

The first step is to accept that your choices and beliefs have brought you to where you are now. You are in charge of your own life. The phrases that will undermine your desire to consciously design a life worth living are phrases such as: "I have to," "I must," "I should," "I need to." These are common phrases, yet they are the very words that keep us in a victim mentality where we fail to acknowledge the power we hold within us. **We always have a choice.** Let me repeat this. We *always* have a choice. We may not always like our choices, but, the truth remains; we always have them. Even prisoners have a choice in how they view their circumstances. The power of a person's imagination can transport them to a new "emotional location" any moment they decide to.

Taking responsibility requires that we use new phrases to consistently remind us of the power we hold. The most useful phrases are: "I would like to," "I want," and "I appreciate." **The most important phrase of all is "I choose."** Why? Because each time you use this phrase you are letting your subconscious and conscious mind know that you have the freedom to choose differently any time you want.

You are the artist of your today and tomorrow. What you choose to do today impacts you, your children, your family, and your community. Any time you don't like what is happening you are free to choose differently—to respond differently. I invite you to make wise choices— choices that support your effort to design a life worth living, with joy, love, and peace.

Chapter Tips:

1. Consciously designing your life requires that you find out what it is that you really want.

2. Going after your dreams means having more to give to your children, becoming a Mom who is fun to be around and providing a model for what your children can become too!

3. You always have a choice—every second, every minute, and every day!

Taking Action:

1. Write out your very own "Wish Upon a Star 100 List" in a keepsake journal and look it over once a day for the next week.

2. Find or create some inspiring affirmations and commit to using them for at least a month. Write your affirmations out 20 times each day and repeat them to yourself whenever you think of it. Write the affirmations you choose here:

   _____

   _____

   _____

   _____

3. What is one thing you would love to do, but haven't done for a long time? Schedule a time to do it within the next month. Stick to it! Call up a girlfriend and ask her to hold you accountable for getting it done.

Dear Diary,

My heart wept the first time I met my client "Karla."
Originally from Mexico, this single mother escaped an
abusive marriage of two years after her husband gave her
a concussion. Karla is a survivor. She moved with her
four-month-old daughter and three-year-old son to a new
country with no friends, little money and is doing her
best to learn conversational English.

On XMAS Eve, when she realized that there would be no
feast to share with loved ones, she went to the bathroom
and locked the door. She turned on the fan and cried from
deep in her belly. Minutes later the doorbell rang. If it
hadn't been for Bernie, her three year old, pleading with
her to answer the door she may have never answered it.
They opened the door together and Karla said she instantly
burst into tears all over again. But this time—they were
tears of joy. Their next-door neighbor was standing
before them holding a cake that said, "Feliz Navidad."
That night they celebrated.

This happened two weeks ago, and Karla shared with me
today in her broken English, "Kelly, that night I remember
what my mother told me. She say there always good when
we keep heart open and give what we have. I do have love
to get and love to give."

So many in our community are starving for connection.
When we lose this, we lose ourselves. It takes relatively
little to reach out but it means ever so much.

Kelly

CHAPTER FOUR

HOW TO UTILIZE YOUR COMMUNITY TO RAISE YOUR CHILD WELL

Is Your Independence Robbing You and Your Kids of an Amazing Life?

They say, "It takes a village to raise a child." Yet, most of us live in "urban jungles" that little resemble the enchantment of a quaint village where the cows moo happily, children play outside safely, and everyone knows each other by name. The irony is that people who live close together in cities often "feel" less close in their hearts. Our modern society values a "rise to the top on your own" attitude, failing to realize that human beings are social animals. It is not intended that we live our lives in isolation, but rather, in communities where we assist one another to survive and thrive!

No matter where you live, how many neighbors you know by name, or how many great people live on your block, being too independent prevents you from accepting the gifts a community can provide your family. If you are under the delusion that you can actually live happily without anyone's help, you are missing out—big time! **Using your independence as a "psychological moat" to keep others from accessing your heart, may be the very barrier that repels those who want to be there for you and your family.**

Breaking through this barrier requires that we take a deep breath and muster up courage to start letting others in! Now, before you start sending out the "Will you be a part of my community?" invites, let's discuss the best way of attracting and keeping quality people in our lives. First things first. You need to be a likeable person. **Regardless of how much you know, how much you make, and how pretty your dimples may be; if you don't show interest in others you will fall flat on your "tush" when it comes to establishing a solid community.**

Some psychological experts have even included "community" as a basic proponent of their philosophies. Alfred Adler based much of his philosophy on the concept called *gemeinschaftsgefühl*—developing a sense of community feeling. The famous Dale Carnegie focuses on developing the skill of being actively interested in others in his *How to Win Friends and Influence People* material to build a stronger community of support.

If you haven't yet noticed—people like talking about themselves. Don't you just love people who take great interest in you? Aren't they just the most charming people? But are you a woman who tends to be the one asking the questions or giving all the answers? When establishing relationships with people in your community you will increase your likeability when you both share and take an active interest in others. This is the secret to being liked by those who are worth spending time with. Do you inspire people to want to have you in their life?

The Ten Secrets to Being a Likeable Person:
1. The most important secret to being liked is to like yourself!!!
2. Take time out for you, so you have more to genuinely give to others.
3. Use the person's name in conversation often *[hearing one's name is like melted butter on biscuits hot out of the oven!].*
4. Smile at others freely.

5. Accept offers of help.
6. Look for the good in everyone *[including youself!]*.
7. Help others from your heart rather than from obligation.
8. Ask people about the things that they care about the most.
9. Follow up with friends. When you say you are going to do something just do it!
10. Regularly appreciate loved ones.

If some of these behaviors seem a little out of character, move outside your comfort zone and challenge yourself; remember that to *have* a friend you have to *be* a friend. Does doing more on this list mean you will be liked by everyone? It doesn't. But, it almost guarantees that you will be liked by you and this is a most attractive quality! I encourage you to commit to doing one thing from the above list today. How about calling up a friend right now to tell her how much she means to you? By doing this you are modeling for your child ways to create meaningful connections.

Do You Believe You Deserve a Supportive Community?

Despite a charming personality and great intentions there is still one thing that could get in the way of creating a supportive community for you and your family. This is simply a belief that you don't deserve wonderful things, experiences and relationships. Many women, Moms, and girls are playing small in this world; believing they do not deserve the amazing opportunities our world affords. **Many of us have bought into the belief that "good girls" do as they are told, don't make waves, and do what others want them to do. This bill of goods is no more useful than "doggie doo doo" on your favorite high-heel shoe!**

We are so programmed to not blow our own horn that we often fail to recognize what is true about ourselves. Many talented women downplay their strengths while everyone else in the free world can plainly see them. **Being humble does not mean lying! Humility is when we confidently speak the truth: admitting, acknowledging, and accepting our own strengths and freely recognizing the strengths of others.**

I have not been immune to playing small. Up until the last couple of years I never considered myself to be particularly "outdoorsy" or fit [*when growing up, my parents' idea of camping was staying at a four-star hotel!*]. But in adulthood, I met a group of rosy-cheeked, fit, outdoor gals. I started tagging along [*more like puffing along*], with them into the good ol' outdoors. And you know what? I loved it! Even after years of hiking one of the most challenging trails in my area two to three times a week I still didn't consider myself to be athletic. Finally, a dear friend gave me a good shake—and the message got through. So I am now pleased to announce to you that I, Kelly Nault am "outdoorsy" and fit! What are you good at? What do others see as your strengths that you might not readily admit?

Oh, and one last thing: **when someone gives you a compliment, the only appropriate response is "thank you."** A compliment should not instigate a debate in which you do your best to dissuade the other from their position about you—doing your best to convince them that you really aren't that good, that you really don't look that good, or that you really don't deserve the compliment. This is bogus, ladies, and you know it! It is time for all of us to give up this unhealthy habit now!

Friends... How Many do You Really Need?

Moms who have accessed the "Ultimate Mom" within, surround themselves with people who they support and who support them in return. Their friends motivate them to become more of who they already are. Aside from family, friends are the backbone of support that get us through the tough times and add to our most cherished times. How many friends do we really need? Some say, all you need is one true "kindred spirit" with whom you can bear your soul, celebrate your successes and share your pain. Yet, a wise friend and counseling colleague, Suzanne Kyra, believes that we actually need a minimum of five bosom buddies. "Why five?" I asked her. "Because when we really need that listening ear in times of stress one friend can't always be there for us. When we have five, by the time we get down the list one of them is bound to be available." We lead busy lives and connections can be lost quite easily. It is up to you to create and maintain those "gems of friends" that are privileged enough to see your life in full—during both the highs and the lows.

For those of you who have yet to create five "gems of friends," who are part of your "inner circle," who witness the good, bad and magnificent about you, I invite you to ask yourself the following:

- Are my friendships working for me?
- Am I doing what I can to keep contact with my friends?
- Am I open to attracting friends with whom I can share?
- Am I willing to risk sharing more of who I am with the friends I already have?

If you fall into the "pleaser" or "perfectionist" category, opening yourself up to others may be a challenge for you. Admitting that you actually have needs may be foreign and you likely shy away from sharing your bad days with others, doubting that they would ever want to hear about them.

It is important to remember that revealing our imperfections or "negative feelings" does not mean wallowing in them. Acknowledging our feelings simply allows us the opportunity to notice what we don't like, in order to move on to what we do like. The reason so many clients have paid me hundreds of dollars to listen to them is that often, they don't believe anyone in their life would want to hear what they have to say. They are too uncomfortable to share with those they know. **If everyone had a supportive network of at least five "gems of friends" I am convinced that my client list would be cut in half and that Moms, children, and families everywhere would be far happier.**

How to Be the Friend that You Wish to Have

To *have* a supportive friend, you need *to be* a supportive friend. Competition and petty jealousies, especially between women, unravel the very support structure that could turn this world around. The "to get to the top I need to step on others" attitude produces sad hearts, minds, and souls in many a woman. This leads to behaviors that unconsciously destroys friendships among family, friends, and coworkers. Doing life alone means less for all of us!

One of the most powerful gifts we can give as a friend and Mother is the ability to celebrate other's success in style—to give our children and friends emotional standing ovations day after day, moment after moment. When we give ourselves permission to freely express our gratitude, our admiration, and our love, we activate the inspiration within our heart and literally become more beautiful women. This is exactly opposite of what many of us were taught as children. We were taught instead to be first, to be better, and perhaps to even put others down in order to scramble to the top. These beliefs do not support the fabric of friendship nor a harmonious community. It is time to establish a new pattern by supporting ourselves, acknowledging that those destructive feelings do come up, and then letting them go!

How to Surround Your Family with People Who Inspire All of You

Our personal world is made up of those we associate with and those we spend time with. The choices we make regarding our circle of family and friends become the slice of the world we create for ourselves and for our children. A Mother's impression of her community is generally based on who she has allowed into her community and will influence her family greatly. An insightful exercise that illuminates the choices we have made in terms of our personal community is the **"Community Circle" Exercise.**

community circle exercise

Quickly grab a pen and paper and draw the "Community Circle" as seen below. Put your name in the middle and then in the outer circle write down the names of at least ten people who you associate with. Be sure to include coworkers, friends, family members, colleagues, and acquaintances. Place the names of those you spend lots of time with, closest to your name; those you see less often, place further away from your name. Once you have completed this, draw a star around those people whom you feel closest to, supported by, and connected to. Now look at your "Community Circle."

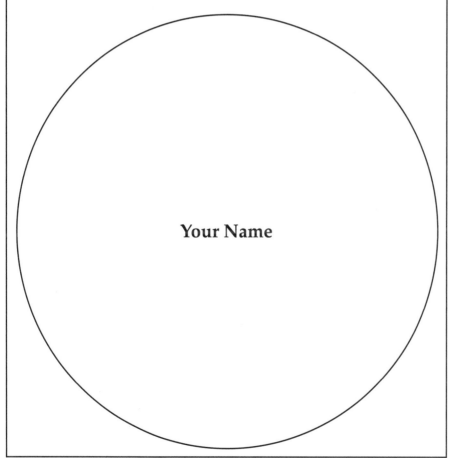

Your Name

What do you notice? Are the "stars" in your life the ones that you spend the most time with? Or do you spend less time with these "star" people? Are there any changes in positions that you would like to make? Would you like to spend more or less time with some of them? Or would you like to attract more "stars" in your life period? You are in the center of this "Community Circle" and have significant power to change the amount of time you spend with many of these individuals. If some of the people you currently have in your life do not empower you, you can choose to improve these relationships, let these "friends" go or begin to spend greater time with the "star" people already in your life. Plus you can create new relationships!

Establishing a healthy community for your children to grow up in, requires that you maintain your power and realize that you make the rules about whom you allow in. One of my favorite quotes is from Susan Taylor who says: "Not everyone is healthy enough to have a front row seat in my life." It is true. **There are millions of people to choose from in this world. Who we associate with can make our days, weeks, months, and years extraordinary or painfully ordinary.** It is up to you to choose. What will you choose to do?

How You Can Establish a Supportive Mom Network

Moms need support like never before. Some Moms have the luxury of frequent breaks, but most don't. Even if you have a nanny, an in-law, or other family member that makes your job easier, establishing friendships with other Moms to create your "Mom Network" is more than just important. I believe it is essential. **Magic occurs for your entire family when you reach out and accept help and support from others.** Sometimes Moms (especially single Moms), get so caught up in their daily tasks that they forget about the bigger picture and don't let people in. I invite you to begin a habit that is "life" giving.

Creating your "Mom Network" can be an important source of support that you won't find anywhere else. For the days that you find yourself smack dab in the middle of the "deep end," other Moms can be invaluable when you call and say, "I don't think I can do it," "I'm scared what I will do or say to them," or bravely ask, "Will you come over and relieve me for half an hour so I can go for a walk?" Aligning yourself with other Moms also provides you with a cost-efficient babysitting program that is based upon exchange of time.

The friends in your "Mom Network" can also be your companions on "girl night outs" and become a source of motivation that inspire you in becoming more of who you seek to become. Napoleon Hill in his timely book, *Think and Grow Rich*, speaks of the power of the "mastermind" group. This is a group that meets on a regular basis and holds you accountable to your dreams, supports you in attaining them, and keeps you on track. Moms bonding together can do this and more! Women are networkers; they can help you find a new hairdresser, new job, or even a new man. This group is ideal for creating an "Ultimate Mom Group" that supports each member in accessing the "Ultimate Mom" within her on a weekly basis. **To find out how you can start your own "Mommy Network" group, go to www.ultimateparenting.com/bookdownloads.**

What Your Kids Learn from Your Acts of Kindness and Unkindness

Like it or not, your kids are watching you more than you will ever know—from how you reach out to others to how you treat strangers on the street. Each time you open the door for someone else in the grocery store, smile and say hello to your neighbor, hold the elevator door open, bring extra food to a food shelter, or give some stranger a compliment, your children are taking notes.

Swear once and they will always remember but do something wonderful and they tend to forget. I used to believe this to be true until walking home from school one day. Out of the blue, Graham asked, "Remember when you told that girl to take her litter out of the pond?" I vaguely recalled that day, it had been over a year. Then Grant laughed and said, "Yeah! She had thrown her binder in the pond and you asked her to fish it out." I had done that. I was upset by the lack of concern this teenage girl showed when she carelessly threw her binder and hundreds of papers in the gorgeous pond that we passed each day. But what amazed me in that moment was the impact it had obviously had on both boys. I was suddenly struck with, "My gosh! What else do they remember?" Humbling, truly!

It is powerful. Moms have the responsibility—like it or not—to create a legacy of memories that can be passed on through the generations. What stories do you have about your parents, grandparents and other loved ones? As a young girl, I knew about one kind act my grandfather performed that I will never forget. My grandpa Ken sent cartoons, jokes and quotes anonymously to a bed-ridden acquaintance. Every week for over a year he would anonymously mail one of these fun surprises to his friend. The friend died without ever knowing it was grandpa who was sending them. It was his widow, who while having tea with my grandmother one day, spotted grandpa's handwriting and made the connection. With tears rolling down her face she said to my grandmother, "You don't know," she sobbed, "What Ken's kindness meant to him. It was the very thing that gave him the courage to keep going." A smile breaks over my face as I share this story with you—a story of how one small kindness can mean the difference between life and death. **It's not about becoming Mother Theresa; it's just doing what we can and what we are inspired to do.** This story is something I am proud to share because it represents the values that I do my best to emulate in my own life. What values are you teaching your child?

Why Building Community is Essential to Your Child's Self-esteem

Lending a helping hand, accepting help from others, and getting your kids involved in a loving community assists in establishing healthy self-esteem. These tasks teach children to be cooperative, respectful, and compassionate. It is these skills that establish what Adlerian psychology calls "social interest"—the sense of oneness and belonging one feels within their primary community. When a child learns to care about others as much as he or she cares for him or herself, that child has acquired the essential ingredient to develop their self-esteem. Self-esteem is the result of feeling good about yourself and being proud of what you can contribute to others. It is not about feeling better than others. It is critical that a child learns to value himself as equal in worth to others.

Dr. Gary McKay, mentor and best-selling author has coined the phrase "people-esteem" to emphasize the often forgotten concept of compassion for others when fostering self-esteem. He states: **"The powerful combination of valuing self and others is what creates a positive sense of contribution and belonging for children. Parents can foster true self-esteem, in which their children also have the 'people-esteem' by modeling basic respect for all others, assisting their children to become part of a broader community and to actively look for ways of helping others."**

The Top Five Volunteer Projects for You and Your Kids

You'd be amazed at how volunteering for a worthwhile charity program will naturally improve your child's "people-esteem." Volunteering with your children is one of the easiest and most rewarding ways to establish a renewed sense of community and it also fosters new skills in your children. Grant and Graham, being blind, have been the recipients of many charitable gifts from Lion's Societies to local banks. At an early age, we knew that it would be important to have them contribute to their community rather than always receiving. They have played the piano at retirement homes, handed out handmade poems to people in the hospital *[make certain you read the one Grant wrote for me in the back of the book to get a sense of his talent!]*, and cleaned up litter at their local high school. The more you get your kids involved in choosing the charity the more excited they will tend to be. **For further information on volunteering go to www.ultimateparenting.com/bookdownloads.**

Five Fun Family Volunteer Projects:

1. **Animal Shelter Volunteers**—Many Animal Shelters run with the help of their volunteers. From dog walking, to fundraising, to grooming—this is a worthy cause that most kids love.

2. **Visit a Retirement Home in Your Area**—There are some residents in retirement homes that are left without visitors for long periods of time. Your kids will get a huge charge out of bringing them balloons, reading to them, or even performing for them.

3. **Hospital Pet Volunteer Programs**—If you have a pet at home this is an excellent way to do some good work in your community. Check into these programs at your local hospital.

4. **Volunteer with an Elderly Person in Your Neighborhood**—Choose an older person in your neighborhood to help out on a consistent basis. Whether it be by purchasing their groceries, taking out their garbage, or raking their leaves you and your kids can be a big help!

5. **Litter Bug Volunteers**—Litter is a problem in many neighborhoods, parks, and schoolyards. Consider combining fun walks with picking up litter. Make a game out of seeing how much garbage you can pick up.

What You Can Learn from Your Kids About Saving the Planet

Children today are far more socially aware and responsible than most of us ever were. They instinctively know that in order to have a future to look forward to, we need to take care of our precious planet. They are often inspired by environmental projects, which can fulfill their desire to be a part of the solution to our world problems. Supporting your children in making this kind of difference supports their zest for life and gives them a deep sense of purpose. Kids may come up with fantastic ideas ranging from organizing your family's recycling system, to wanting to have a garage sale, to using more environmentally friendly products.

Encourage them to learn more and to take responsibility for the initiatives they want to implement. Share in their enthusiasm—you'll never know where it will take you, your children, and our planet.

Essential "Life Field Trips" for You and Your Kids

Volunteer experience and home recycling programs are ways to expose your children to their community and help them to assist others. Yet, the natural desire to protect your kids can prevent you from exposing them to the opportunities of our world. Broadening their sense of the world is what often keeps them safer in the long run. If you don't, the media will. **This** can be very dangerous as the media misleads children when it comes to sex, drugs, and violence. How do you expand their view of the world? Introduce them to different cultures, people, and lifestyles. Educational programs, books and especially "life field trips" can also accomplish this expanded global view. What are "life field trips?" These trips are ways in which kids can experience other walks of life.

Three Essential "Life Field Trips":

1. **Go to a Different Economic Area of Town.** Drive your kids through the wealthier and poorer areas of town. Ask them questions about what they think of these areas and watch your own biases. These conversations may occur as you are driving. Don't worry if your children aren't that interested; often, they will bring it up later.
2. **Visit a Different Cultural Area of Town.** Experiencing different cultures expands a child's world and enhances compassion, understanding, and tolerance of others: qualities that will establish success in their future. Explore a different ethnic area of town by going into shops, learning a few of the words like "hello" and "thank you", and eating the local food. If you live on an island or in a rural town expose your child to urban cultures while on vacation. These experiences can go a long way in supporting your child to develop tolerance and open-mindedness.

> 3. **Tour Your Local Animal Shelter.** Discuss what happens to
> the animals if they are not taken care of. How do the animals
> act if they have been abused? These lessons will help support
> your children in being both considerate and compassionate.

Other field trips could include camping outdoors, going to a farm (especially for city kids), or traveling anywhere and everywhere. When we only stick with what we know we can miss out on so much. Opening your children's eyes to the world not only keeps them safe, but also gives them more to dream about in their future!

Chapter Tips:

1. Three ways to be an amazing and likeable woman is to show interest in others, to share what is in our own heart and to smile often!

2. True "gems of friends" are the ones who know how to celebrate our successes in style and are appreciative when we do the same!

3. Modeling for your child how to be kind, to do for others and be compassionate is what will nurture their true self-esteem—"people-esteem."

Taking Action:

1. Choose one person that you want to spend more time with. Call them up today and make plans to see them sometime in the next month.

2. Talk to your children about volunteering. Research and brainstorm possible opportunities for you to contribute as a family.

3. If you created your very own "Mom Network": Which women would you want in your group? What would they be like and how would you help one another?
   Contact a woman today whom you would like in your group to share your ideas with. Write down the names of women you would like to contact here:

   _____

   _____

   _____

   _____

Dear Diary,

If I doubted the importance of "family meetings" before,
I no longer doubt them. Today in my parenting class,
a father named "Jacob" shared an inspiring story.
His family has started to use "family meetings" with success.
When their favorite aunt died suddenly two weeks ago, they
called a "family meeting" and invited their extended family
to join in. The air was both tense and sad because everyone
had their own idea of what their beloved aunt would
have wanted.

But Jacob's nine-year-old Samantha saved that day!
During the meeting she shared a conversation that she
had had with her Aunt while walking to the park only
three months earlier. They happened to talk about dying
that day—what happens when we die and what she would
want others to do when she died. Instantly, they came
to a decision. Everyone was relieved that the process
of coming together had given Samantha the voice that
empowered all of them with information that they
knew their aunt would have approved of.

"Family meetings" are powerful. Every time family
members come together as equal contributing members,
you are increasing the odds of everyone feeling loved,
appreciated and valued. These are odds I would bet on
any day!

Kelly

GIVE EVERYONE
IN YOUR HOME WHAT
THEY WANT
INCLUDING
YOU!

How to Build Trust that Makes or Breaks Your Kid!

Trust is an essential part of a solid home and is something that is important to each member of the family. There is a story that someone shared with me once that I would like to share with you:

> Jamie comes home one day from school to find dad waiting impatiently at the door. "Come in here, Jamie. I want to teach you something. I've decided it is time for you to learn about trust. What I want you to do is to stand on the fireplace mantel and fall straight back into my arms. I promise to catch you." After a couple of minutes of prodding, Jamie steps up on the mantel, closes his eyes, takes a deep breath, and falls backward just as dad steps out of the way to let Jamie smash to the ground. Shocked, hurt and confused Jamie cries out, "Why did you do that? You said you were going to catch me!" Dad sneers, "Lesson number one about trust: don't ever, ever, trust anybody!"

Such a brutal story! Thank goodness most parents would never even think of breaking a child's trust in such an obvious and mean-spirited way. Unfortunately, we sometimes break our kids trust without evening knowing it. Breaking promises by not keeping our word, speaking badly about our children in the heat of anger, and using punishment such as spanking, slapping, and grounding only breeds mistrust. These actions do not leave physical bruises like the ones Jamie suffered, but the emotional scarring will follow them into their future. Children who lack trust have difficulty forming intimate relationships, see life as a glass half-empty, and often see the world as a scary place. They avoid risk. Since there are no guarantees in life, failing to risk seals their fate of a life not lived. This chapter is intended to support you in building a solid foundation of trust, which will nurture everyone in the family—including you!

How You can Establish Trust in Your Home

Despite their differences, each member of your family wants to live in a trusting home where they feel they belong and where what they have to offer is important. Fostering a supportive environment such as this occurs when your kids are:

1. Trusted.
2. Respected.
3. Listened to (without judgment).

Building trust is an essential element in building a safe home where your children are encouraged to risk, where their mistakes are welcomed (as opportunities to learn), and where they know they are valued. Trust, respect, and listening are the cornerstones of heart-felt communication: one of the most important ways to experience joy and love. Establishing trust requires that you model for your child trusting behavior by following through on your word, helping others, keeping secrets, respecting yourself, respecting your child [yes, this means no diary reading!], and honoring other's feelings. When you successfully model trust you will produce a triple WIN for you, your child, and your relationship.

Four Benefits of the "Family Meeting" You Won't Want to Miss

Trust to a family is like oxygen to a body. One of the best ways to maintain a home that fosters trust is to use the "family meeting." If you have attempted "family meetings" in the past and have experienced disappointment, I encourage you to read this section with an open mind.

"Family meetings" can be difficult at first and yet, if you follow the simple format below, these meetings can provide a family with an avalanche of positive benefits including:

- **Creates a team approach in which each family member feels respected.** This creates a bond of confidence that will assist your family in supporting one another and working through conflict.

- **Teaches your children leadership skills in a fun and rewarding way.** This is "real-time" school at its best. Learning as a child how to chair a meeting, cooperate with others, resolve conflict, and become an active listener is powerful. These skills can do more for your child's future than their resumé.

- **Ensures that everyone, including you Mom, feels heard.** One of the most important ways to love your children is by listening to them. When children know that their opinions matter, they do not need to resort to using revenge, rebellion or other misbehaviors to be heard.

- **Reduces conflict quickly and effectively.** "Family meetings" can buy you precious time when you're busy or stressed. When you don't have an immediate response to your child's problems, simply tell them to add the issue to the "family meeting agenda" and solve it then. You won't believe how much time and aggravation this one act will save! The best part? Sometimes your child will find a solution long before the meeting.

How to Be Certain Your "Family Meetings" Don't Turn into "Bored Meetings"

Remember it is a "family meeting" not a "bored meeting!" To get your kids and significant other on board, the meetings need to be FUN, FUN, FUN! If you do not include fun, your meetings will become a forum for complaints. If this happens your meetings will be extremely short lived!

So how do you make meetings fun? The more you get your children involved the more fun the meetings tend to be. Ask your kids what would make the meeting fun. Brainstorm these ideas and come up with ways for "family meetings" to work for everyone. Take turns choosing a fun family activity at the end of each meeting. Some ideas include: movie nights, a bike rides together, tickling fights, ice cream outings, playing games, making cookies, or going for walks. Other fun activities that can be incorporated into the meetings include: a family chant, song, cheer, or handshake. Get creative and watch the fun naturally unfold!

The Simplest "Family Meeting" Guideline

Consistency is key to establishing successful "family meetings." Setting a specific day and time each week can be challenging, especially for Moms and dads who have inconsistent schedules. Make it as consistent as you possibly can and choose a day that leaves flexibility to do something as a family afterwards. Sundays are often the best choice.

Your "Family Meeting" Guideline:

1. **Take Turns Fulfilling the Roles**. These roles are:
   - Host—Provides beverages.
   - Chairperson—Opens the meeting and follows the set agenda.
   - Secretary—Keeps the minutes in a family book (either written or with pictures).
   - Timer—Ensures the meeting stays on track and does not go into the wee hours of the night.

2. **Ensure that Everyone is Heard.** Each family member has the right to add any issues to the agenda that they wish. Keep a paper or envelope on your fridge where everyone can add items for discussion throughout the week.

3. **Stick Close to the Time Schedule.** Choose shorter amounts of time for younger kids (15 minutes) and gradually increase the length of time as their attention span increases (45 minutes—1 hour). If there are too many issues to cover, carry

them over to the following week. Schedule a certain amount of time for each issue and watch the timer. When you put your mind to it, you can often cover an issue just as well in 15 minutes as you can in an hour.

4. **Stay Flexible.** Do not get hung up on the format. If young kids wander away from the table that's OK. Have them partake in what's interesting for them. Encourage their involvement by giving them a role and adapt when necessary. For instance if they are the secretary and have not yet learned to write, have them draw a picture of the "family meeting."

5. **Include Allowances and Family Rituals.** Start and end your meetings with a meaningful ritual like those described in the next section. Go over allowances *[see Chapter Fourteen]* and find solutions to any issues on the agenda. Remember always sandwich "issues" between fun rituals.

Rituals Worth Including in Your "Family Meeting"

Kids love rituals! Rituals provide "warm fuzzies" for the entire family and are a special aspect of the "family meeting." Here are some rituals that I have used:

- **"Thank You Fors"**—Take turns sharing what you are thankful for. When you are finished pass to another by saying, "I pass to _____*(name)*." Once everyone has had the opportunity to share, the last person states, "I pass to regular conversation." This one ritual guides the family to focus on the positive aspects of life and it gives everyone a chance to share uninterrupted. To keep interruptions to a minimum some families use a "talking stick" in which they agree that only the person holding the stick speaks.

- **Appreciations: "Something I Appreciate About You is _____"**—This exercise guides your family to focus on one another's strengths: especially important for siblings who seem to enjoy putting one another down. Whoever goes first chooses a family member to honor and says, "Something I appreciate about you is _____." Take turns until everyone has been honored at least once. Appreciations are especially useful as they encourage each family member with words of kindness. Don't worry if it first doesn't go well. Stay positive and model for your children how to be specific when giving their appreciations.

- **"Cheese and Whine"**—This exercise was inspired by Dr. Phil's, "Would you like some cheese with that whine" comment. When there is a lot of complaining in a home I suggest using this exercise. Each family member has a chance to share all the things that really annoy him or her. Use a two-minute egg timer to ensure your whining time is limited and focused. Encourage your child to use up all their time and recommend that they share in the whiniest voice possible. This usually results in peals of laughter and quickly breaks the pattern of negativity.

- **"Chicken Soup for the Soul Moments"**—Jack Canfield and Mark Victor Hansen wrote a book called *Chicken Soup for the Kid's Soul*. We used to start each morning with one of the inspiring stories from that book to set us up for a positive day. Taking turns reading and sharing a positive story at the beginning or end of the "family meeting" leaves everyone feeling inspired, grateful, loved and connected.

How to Create Quality Time When Cooking at Home

In addition to providing time for rituals, "family meetings" are an excellent time to set a weekly meal schedule and write out the grocery list. Family members can also make special meal requests and choose their nights to help you make dinner *[if it is not every night already!]*. And yes, husbands are to be included! Start involving everyone in the process now—from grocery shopping to preparation. The earlier you start, the better! Young children are often thrilled to set the table and play the role of "sous-chef;" pulling things out of the fridge for you. Preparing meals as a family also provides daily quality time together that you might otherwise miss out on. Grant and Graham would alternate between helping me prepare dinner and setting the table. During this time together, they put on their favorite music and we would sing, visit, and sometimes even dance! Note that children in their tweens and teens may choose to make dinner on their own. Taking this step to involve your children increases their appreciation as they experience first-hand the time and effort that goes into meals. Making dinner may become your favorite time of the day! So what's for dinner tonight, Mom?

What to Do When No One Shows Up for the "Family Meeting"

After hearing about all the benefits of "family meetings" you may have a beautiful vision of your entire family singing *Kumbaya* around the kitchen table. But what if no one shows up when you call the first meeting? This is exactly what happened to one Mom. At her first "family meeting" no one showed up—out of her three kids—not a one decided to attend. Her husband didn't even make an appearance! Instead of "making" them show up, she decided to go ahead and have the meeting on her own. She made herself a cup of coffee, went over the agenda, and started making decisions. During the week, when one of her children would ask, "When did you make that decision Mom?" she would happily reply, "Oh, at our last 'family meeting'." She continued to invite the family to attend and used the time to set her goals and have an undisturbed cup of coffee. Slowly, over the course of a couple of months, her entire family chose to attend. The moral of this story—be patient, if it doesn't work the first time keep the faith and enjoy the meeting solo!

How to Involve Your Kids in Finding Solutions to Family Problems

So far "family meetings" sound like a dream and yet, what do you do when there are problems? Problems have received a bad reputation as something to be avoided. In reality, they are marvelous opportunities in disguise. **Viewing problems as a chance for you and your children to grow can positively transform the way you deal with them.** What are the benefits of problems? Often not much! But what if problems actually encouraged us to try something new, inspired us to brainstorm solutions, stretched us to become more than what we are now—to break out of our comfort zone and expand? If this was the case, would you begin to look at problems differently, even welcome them? With all these benefits you'd be crazy not to!

So how can we begin to use problems as a way to work toward peaceful resolution? The easiest way is to choose to see problems differently—as an opportunity to focus on solutions and involve your kids in the process. This helps children feel respected and can bring you closer together as a result. It is important to note that including your children does not mean that you will do exactly what they say—all it means is that you will hear them, listen from your heart, and consider it. **When dealing with family problems it is essential to focus you and your kids on what it is you both truly want, rather than on what it is you don't want.** The main goal is to seek an agreeable solution that respects everyone rather than finding fault and blame.

How to Use "Family Meetings" to Deal with Conflict

Is treating conflict as an opportunity to learn, new to you? If so, you are not alone! Ever feel sick when arguing, or when on the verge of a disagreement? To this day, a pit in my stomach can develop during times of conflict. Most of us have been there; an emotional day makes the irrational appear completely rational. We believe we are right and justified! During these moments, many of us overtly (or covertly) "draw a line in the sand" and tell our children that they are wrong—that what they feel is wrong. Not only does this hurt our children, conflict can be disease producing when Moms remain silent, lash out, or emotionally shut down over time.

Telling the truth—the real truth—is the door that opens our hearts to receiving and giving unconditional love in difficult situations. **Resolving conflict happens naturally when we acknowledge our feelings, look for solutions, and choose to become closer by listening to one another.** Successful "family meetings" are the result of encouraging our child's fears and hurts to be expressed. Discuss with your kids how you want to handle conflict in your family and create a "Family Deep End Oath," which can be used when one (or all of you!) are headed for the "deep end." During each meeting, take turns reading this oath out loud to remind you of your commitment especially when dealing with those heated topics. Have each member sign your "Family Deep End Oath" and place it in a central location of your home.

Sample "Family Deep End Oath":

1. We focus on what we like about one another.
2. We are specific when we talk about our problems.
3. We take responsibility for what we do and what we can do to change.
4. We are honest.
5. We breathe deeply to help move through our feelings.
6. We forgive one another.
7. We ask for forgiveness and apologize when appropriate.
8. We use the "talking stick" and listen carefully.
9. We look for solutions in order to become closer.
10. We look for ways to love one another more deeply.

"Family Meetings" at Their Best

"Family meetings" can become a tradition that is passed down through the generations. Having everyone contribute happens with time, with patience and with a bit of fun. In addition to regular weekly meetings, holiday planning and family goal planning can also be incorporated. Whatever you choose to incorporate in your meetings can become the backbone of your family in which conflict is cleared up peacefully and on a regular basis. "Family meetings" can resolve misunderstandings, build trust, and encourage self-confidence more than any other tool.

It is now up to you... when will you have your "family meeting?"

Chapter Tips:

1. To ensure your "family meetings" do not turn into "bored meetings" always include time for sharing, for fun, and for play!

2. Rituals like "Thank You Fors," "Appreciations," and "Chicken Soup For The Soul Moments" establish trust and connection for your entire family.

3. The first step to resolving conflict is realizing that often, family members ultimately want the same thing—to feel cherished, appreciated and respected.

Taking Action:

1. Choose a day to schedule your "family meeting" and decide to enjoy it even if you are the only person who shows up. Write down the best day for a "family meeting" in your household here:

_____

2. Brainstorm fun family rituals that the whole family wants to try and start using them. Some of the rituals I would like to incorporate are:

_____

_____

_____

_____

_____

_____

3. Actively involve the entire family in preparing family meals. List your ideas here:

_____

_____

_____

_____

_____

_____

_____

_____

Dear Diary,

Yipppeeee! Just received an email from Kathy who shared
how the sibling rivalry techniques in my book transformed
a fight between Nicholas, her four year old, and Sam,
her two year old. "

The other day the boys were fighting over whose favorite
video they were going to watch. I encouraged them
to take turns. But no go. It was 'I want to watch mine!'
So, I said, 'Okay, while you are deciding, we'll listen
to music.' I put on a CD, which they usually love,
but they cried and were mad at each other."

Later Sam & I were at the kitchen table and Nicholas
went up to Sam and said, 'Sam I want to talk to you.'
and Sam said, 'No Nicholas, go away!' Nicholas walked
away and then came back and said in a very emotional
voice, 'Sam, I just came over to talk to you because
I wanted to say I'm sorry for hurting your feelings but
you hurt my feelings too.' And do you know what Sam
said? 'Thank-you Nedowley.' which is how he says Nicholas.
It was beautiful and I sat with tears in my eyes
watching. It was amazing and I told them both that
I was so proud of them. We never did watch their videos.
Instead we danced in the living room!'"

Even after hearing hundreds of success stories like this one
I am still awed by the effectiveness of these tools and am
inspired by the courage Mothers show in using them.

Kelly

What every mom ought to know about Solving Sibling Rivalry

How Can Kids from the Same Family be So Different?

Have you ever wondered how children from the same family can be so different? Ever wondered why you and your siblings are the opposite of one another in some or all areas of your personality and skill? Perhaps, you were even convinced as a child, that your sibling was adopted and actually told them that they were switched in the hospital at birth. Time and time again, I will surprise parents by correctly guessing which siblings in their family are most different after having only been given their children's sex, names and ages. "How did you know?" they ask. Simple! **It is because of what I call the "Law of Siblings," which states that the closer children are in age the more different they tend to be (especially when they are the same sex).** Does this apply to all siblings? Although there are exceptions to the rule, it does apply to the vast majority of families.

Why does the "Law of Siblings" apply so often? It is because we all want to find our own way to belong—to have our place in the world. Since our society reveres competition, siblings often come to the mistaken conclusion that only one person in the family can be the "best" at any particular skill. Therefore, in order to belong they need to be different than the other. **Siblings often compare themselves to one another and if one is the "best" at something, the other will strive to be "the best at** being the worst." If one is the "academic" the other will be the "athlete" or "artist." These roles are not written in stone, and can actually change over time. For instance, if the one who has been at the top of their class starts letting their grades slide you may very well see the other pick up their socks and suddenly "ace" a few tests.

But what about those siblings who do share similar interests and skills? What about the *Jackson Five* who were all talented musically? When we find children from the same family who are close in age, of the same sex, and have similar interests and talents you will often find that they were raised in a family or culture that valued team work above personal success. It is also highly probable that the children's parents value this specific skill or talent.

Why Being an "Only," "Youngest," "Eldest," and "Middle" Has Everything to do with Their Behavior

When children are born, they are instantly born into a particular birth order: the only, the eldest, the second, the middle, the youngest or the multiple. With every birth you change the family dynamic. Children also interpret their place in the family differently and the interpretations they make impact their behavior.

For example, imagine you are an only child born into a lovely family—just you, your Mom and your dad *[sigh]*. Quite heavenly really! It is wonderful being the "Little Prince" or "Little Princess" of the family and you just know you belong because you are the center of attention and the "apple of your parents' eye." But suddenly there is anarchy, your throne is threatened and you are not prepared. A new baby has actually had the audacity to show up and demand your parents' attention! What the heck has happened to your parents? Suddenly they are serving this "thing!" They say this "thing" is your sibling—your flesh and blood—but to you this "thing" is merely crowding your turf. Your relatives are thrilled with this new "bundle of joy"—bearing presents and dying to look at it, hold it, and cuddle it. This is not a happy time in your life. So what do you do? How do you get their attention back?

It is very common for the eldest child in this situation to suddenly start talking baby talk, mistakenly believing that the way to belong is to act like the baby. But this only backfires as they quickly learn that the "baby" has this helpless behavior down pat. Soon they realize that they simply cannot compete. The eldest child will often change strategy and will secure his or her place in the family by striving to be the "first" and "best" in most situations.

Eldest children are not the only ones with mistaken interpretations that impact their behavior. Below you will find general descriptions of each birth order that may give you a better understanding of your children and maybe even of your own siblings! Keep in mind that these are just guidelines and are not written in stone.

The Typical Qualities and Behaviors for Each Birth Order are as Follows:

- **Only Child**—Only children often live in a strictly "adult setting," rarely have children to play with in their home and thus, can have difficulty sharing. Depending upon their parents' style, they become either independent or dependent. They are often achievement oriented, are used to getting their own way and are accustomed to being the center of their parents' universe. A stubborn streak can be the result of habitually getting their way *[as an only child myself, no comment here! ☺]*.

- **Eldest Child**—Eldest children strive to be "the best" at all they do. They are often the "academic" of the family, placing high standards on themselves to succeed and are responsible, conforming to family rules more than the others. They enjoy being in control of situations and of others. They are not known to be the best risk takers.

- **Second Child**—Second born children are the "rule breakers" who question rules and regulations. They struggle to keep up and attempt to exceed the eldest in everything they do. Often, they find their place by being good at whatever the eldest is not. Frequently, they appear to require less of their parents' attention and are more flexible and easy-going.

- **Middle Child**—A true "middle child" is born into families of four or more children. They are often sensitive and act as a "negotiator"—trying to bring everyone together. Sometimes they view life at home as unfair. Often more social, they reach out to the community. At times they feel left out and can either be the strongest or weakest personality within the family.

- **Youngest Child**—The "baby" of the family often enjoys "Prince" or "Princess-like" status. They are rarely quiet and make their presence known by doing whatever it takes to get the attention of others. By acting helpless or cute, they often manipulate other members of the family to do things for them that they could do for themselves. They enjoy play and are known to strive to do better than their other siblings.

- **Multiples (also known as "twins")**—Most often, multiples will be clear on who is older and who is younger. Even when their "age" only differs by minutes they will often act accordingly to the birth order descriptions as described above.

Are there exceptions to the rule? Absolutely! Birth order is only a guideline and is not the deciding factor. It is the interpretations made by your child about his or her role in your family and in your community that will determine their choices in life. These interpretations can change over time especially when: a) a family uses proactive parenting techniques supporting every child to belong and to contribute as a team member; b) one sibling surpasses another by becoming better in a particular area and they appear to switch birth orders; c) a child has a long-term illness, mental or physical disability that results in them being treated like the youngest child; d) when an unusual event or set of circumstances has a significant impact on a child's sense of security; e) and if there are more than seven years between the children, the above birth order guidelines will not apply.

Competition and What a Mom Can Do About it

Much of the personality differences in birth order are the result of unhealthy competition. Do parents contribute to unhealthy competition? You bet! Many families today create a "black sheep" in the family without even realizing they are doing so. The language used by parents to praise their children often has the underlying message of "When you do it like your sister/brother I love you." or worse yet, "When you don't do it like your sister/brother I do not love you." It is often subtle, but other times, it is not so subtle. Whenever a Mom thinks, "Why can't you just be more like your brother?" or "Why can't you be more like your sister?" it is time to focus on the strengths of the child you are having a challenge with. Comparison only puts your children down and creates greater conflict in the end.

Eldest children, usually conforming to the rules of the family, often identify themselves as the "good one," while their sibling becomes the "bad one." This dynamic establishes unhealthy self-esteem as the "good one" begins to equate their worth with being better than the other. The eldest may begin to use subtle (and not so subtle) putdowns of the younger sibling focusing on their faults. **The problem with linking one's self-confidence to being better than someone else is that it is impossible to be the best at everything—you will always find someone better, prettier, or more skilled than you.** When a child believes that their position as "best," "favorite," and "number one," is being threatened by a sibling, the drive to get to the top can create much needless pressure.

It is common for children to compare themselves to one another; it happens all the time in our homes, schools, and communities. This past year, I played a children's board game with "Jody" and her friend "Samantha." Jody, having played the game numerous times, was very skilled in the math portion of the game. Samantha struggled with each math question saying things like, "I'm so bad at math." Jody would proudly answer all of Samantha's math questions for her. Unconsciously, Jody was creating an experience where Samantha felt less and less confident. Finally, I said to Jody, "Because you have had so much experience with the game let's help Samantha improve her game by supporting her to answer the math problems on her own." Jody, an eldest child, was not thrilled by my suggestion as it took away from her feeling "special." Soon Samantha was answering the math problems with confidence and at the end of the game I said to her, "What a quick math learner you are!" She beamed. When her Mom came to pick her up that night she literally jumped into her arms and proudly shared her success! **It is time for us to teach our children that part of being "special" means helping others to succeed, rather than putting others down to prove our worth.**

Is it Possible that You Favor One Child Over Another?

Favoritism, although common, is one more thing that can lead to unnecessary competition. When one child is better at something than another, [*especially when that something is listening to one's parents!*], it is easy to favor them. It is so much easier to feel connected to the one who does what you want them to do. Yet this can become a destructive pattern that fosters a phony kind of self-esteem based upon being better than others.

There have been many times when the boys have put one another down and have wanted me to know just how "bad" the other was. There also have been many times when I favored one over the other. While Graham was extremely quiet as a young child, answering most questions with "OK" and "fine," I sometimes found it difficult to connect with him. Yet, at other times while triggered by Grant's misbehavior, I felt closer to Graham. Finally, I got it! All I needed to do was actively focus on the other's strengths and spend quality time with that one. Now whenever I start to feel a deep connection with one boy over the other, I know it is time for me to make an extra effort to connect with the other. After a sincere attempt, it currently takes me less than a couple of fun hours on a "special date" to reconnect once again. **It is natural, when we are feeling annoyed or frustrated to want to pull away. The secret lies in having the courage to take a leap toward the other child in order to reconnect, rather than maintaining emotional angst by distancing ourselves.**

The Secret that Youngest Born Do Not Want You to Know!

Is there anything else Moms need to know about siblings? Lots! There is a secret that I want to share with you now. You may be surprised to find that millions of youngest children around the world have a secret they have kept hidden from their Moms for years. I warn you! Once you know their secret you will never be able to look at sibling rivalry the same way again. It can also be the catalyst for you to successfully deal with sibling conflicts, which take up so much of your time and energy. Ready? Shhhhh! **The secret is this—more times than not, youngest children are the ones who actually instigate the fights! And they do this right under your nose, but you never know because they will quickly blame their older brother or sister for starting it.** It is a game that provides great fun for them especially when all they have to do is to turn on the waterworks (tears) to effectively get your attention. And while you are comforting them, they can gleefully look over your shoulder at their older sibling and claim victory with a smile that says, "Gotcha!" Moms across the nation blindly walk right into this game. And who do you punish? You got it—the older one. Why? "Because they should of known better." What to do about it? Read on!

The Hidden Purpose of Sibling Fights and How to Stop Them

Sibling fights are an annoying part of your day that impacts the entire family. When the tears start to roll a Mom can feel responsible to stop it! Yet fighting, like it or not, can actually give children the sense of belonging and connection they seek. When siblings fight in close proximity of their parents, it is almost certain that they are seeking their parents' attention. Younger siblings will intentionally find ways to bug their older siblings for the sole purpose of receiving attention.

It's confession time! Isn't it true that instead of having faith in our kids to solve their own fights, we jump right in and get involved? **We literally jump right into the "fighting ring" with our children by:**

- Yelling, "How many times do I have to tell you?"
- Physically separating the kids and sending them each for a "time-out."
- Comforting one while punishing the other: "Come here sweetie!" and to the other, "You should know better!"
- Refereeing the situation by telling them how to solve it.

Getting Involved in Sibling Fights has the Following Consequences:

- It rewards their fighting behavior and actually gives them the attention they seek.
- It takes away the opportunity to learn how to get along, to meet their own needs, and to resolve conflict on their own.
- It causes Mom stress, frustration, and anger.

Every time you get involved in your children's fights you are unconsciously supporting the very behavior that stresses you out! **The solution? Stay out of the fights, Mom!** "But wait a minute!" you may be saying. "What about when one child is much smaller than the other and needs my protection?" This is a valid concern and an excellent question! Teaching your children ways of handling conflict (at any age) is a life skill that is essential for getting along in the home, school and in the community. Training your children how to stay physically safe is crucial. How do you do this?

The best way in helping your children to step up to the plate and to deal with sibling fights on their own, is to first discuss it. Share with your children that having a peaceful home and keeping them safe is something you value. **Let your children know that when it comes to fights they always have a choice.** Ask them if they are interested in learning how to best deal with their sibling fights so they can feel good. Then share the following "Sibling Fight Strategy."

The Sibling Fight Strategy:

1. **Use Your Words.** Let the other sibling know that they do not choose to fight.
2. **Take a Hike.** Remove oneself from the situation. If the other sibling follows, move to step three.
3. **Find a Safe Place to go.** Find a place where the sibling won't follow: the bathroom with the door locked, their bedroom, or even their parents' room.

Now when the tears and accusations fly at you Mom, simply ask, "What do you need to do?" Saying less is preferrable and will help to keep you out of a debate. If necessary, repeat the same question adding an occasional, "I have faith that you will find a solution," or "Let me know how it goes." Later share, "You must be proud for handling yourself so well."

The Lessons Your Kids Learn while Fighting

Since fighting always takes two, it stands to reason that if they choose to fight they can also choose to cooperate and get along. Sharing the "Sibling Fight Strategy" with your children and encouraging them to use it empowers them. Your kids will gain considerable confidence when they know they have the freedom and tools to get out of fights whenever they want. Giving your children the opportunity to practice negotiation skills can boost their conflict resolution abilities. These skills can support your children when handling bullying at school, and even later on in the workplace. Mom, this is one of the most valuable skills you can give your children. But it will only work if you let them handle their own fights. Be forewarned that they may do everything in their power to keep you involved, especially if you have had years of doing so! Stay firm. When they come to you crying or complaining because of a fight, ask them, "Did you take a hike and find a safe place to go to?" This is most often the only response that is needed.

You might be skeptical that this approach could ever result in anything other than more fighting. I know I was, but I decided to try it anyway. One afternoon I heard angry screams coming from upstairs and then the youngest, Grant, came running into the room with a tear stained face yelling: "Graham hit me!" I managed to remain calm and say, "I guess that happens when you choose to fight. It's a tough challenge, but I am certain you'll be able to work it out. Let me know how it goes." Stunned, he momentarily stopped crying then began to wail, "But aren't you going to do anything?" I smiled and said, "This is between you and Graham. It's a toughie, but I trust you'll find a way to keep yourself safe. Let me know how it goes."

Although these comments ended this particular fight, only two days later, it appeared that they had forgotten everything. Another big fight exploded into World War III and I could hear screaming once again with Grant shouting, "If you do that one more time I am going to tell Kelly!" To which Graham replied, "Go ahead. You know she'll just tell you to figure it out yourself." Then the magic happened, it got quiet! It was sheer bliss when I realized I had just mastered the lesson: stay out of it. Now, you can choose to do the same.

If there isn't Blood, Chances are You are Not Needed!

Having made my point on the importance of not stepping into the sibling "fighting ring," I now want to discuss those times when you may need to intervene. Many Moms ask, but what if there *is* blood? Great question. If this happens then you will need to get involved. Part of life is learning how to take care of one another especially when we have hurt them. Family counselor, Dr. Oscar Christensen shared a story I have never forgotten. Once one of his children hit the other so hard that stitches were required. Rather than punishing the offending child, Dr. Christensen responded by giving "the hitter" a wet washcloth to hold against the hurt child's wound while they drove in the car to the hospital. Once it was time for the stitches, he allowed "the hitter" to do the handholding. This is an example of using a negative situation to teach a positive lesson. What if we always gave our children the responsibility and opportunity to help with the healing? What would our children learn? These are "teachable moments" that can offer life long lessons. Don't rob your children of the chance to learn some new skills in compassion by doing it for them.

Reduce the Chances of Your Children Becoming Violent

There are not only fights happening in our homes, but violence in our community. Terrorism in our world and bullying in our schools are of real concern today. Some interesting research points to the direct correlation between children watching violent television and children behaving violently. We live in busy times where Moms often do not supervise the selection of their children's TV programs. The result? Children are exposed to more questionable media than ever.

The National Television Violence Study (the largest ongoing scientific study of television violence) concluded that television violence tends to be sanitized, sensationalized, and glamorized resulting in negative impact on children. Dr. Barbara Wilson, senior researcher, states that, "Younger children have difficulty distinguishing televised fantasy from reality, and are therefore at increased risk of imitating cartoon violence." It is estimated that children will see over 100,000 incidents of violence by the time they reach thirteen years of age! According to this study the three major effects of witnessing violence on television are as follows: children become less sensitive to the pain and suffering of others, have an increased fear of the world, and show an increase in aggressive and violent behavior towards others.

Getting ready to throw out your TV? Try the following before your do.

How to Lessen the Impact of Violence and Keep Your TV:

1. Watch a minimum of one whole episode of the programs your child watches so you understand the type of content they will be exposed to.

2. Discuss violent acts that occur during episodes and brainstorm other ways to solve conflict during the commercials or at "family meetings."

3. Ensure that you teach your child to clearly differentiate between reality and fictional TV.

4. Reduce the amount of violence that your child are exposed to by introducing fun alternatives to TV.

5. Encourage your child to watch videos (that you have pre-screened) when you are not around.

6. Foster communication with your child and take time to find out what is going on with them at school.

Chapter Tips:

1. Fostering true self-esteem in your children means supporting them to become their best and inspiring them to help others succeed.

2. Any time you realize that you are favoring one child over another go on a "special date" to reconnect with the child you find challenging.

3. One of the most effective ways to deal with sibling rivalry is to stay out of it!

Taking Action:

1. Support each child in finding ways to end fights easily by using the "Sibling Fight Strategy."

2. Make a pact with yourself to stay out of your children's fights from now on and stick with it!

3. Think about the child you feel less close to right now and schedule some quality time for the two of you.

Dear Diary,

"Darlene," a Mom in the Wednesday night parenting workshop I am facilitating, shared how she has begun to involve her three-year-old, "Tyler," in household chores. Each week, she accompanies him to the laundry room and waits until he has performed his weekly job—transferring the wet clothes from the washer into the dryer. Simple? Yes! Quick? No! She props him on top of the dryer and holds on as he happily leans over the washer and fishes out all the clothes one-at-a-time. She reports that it takes over ten minutes —a job that would easily take her 15 seconds!

Darlene has accessed the "Ultimate Mom" within her, as she is consciously giving her son the opportunity to feel like a valuable contributing member of the household. She respects Tyler, takes time to train him, and is nurturing a child who is beginning to experience the internal benefits of helping out. She also reports that bringing along a magazine is of great help!

Kelly

How to Get Your Kids To Do Their Chores Smiling!

Why Kids Secretly Like Chores!

Despite popular belief, kids secretly like to do chores! "Yeah right! Not my kids," you might be thinking. I know it appears they don't, but deep (sometimes very deep) down they do. So why do they like chores? **Kids want to contribute, period! Doing some of the household maintenance is one of the positive ways in which they can contribute every day.** With the aid of modern technology many household tasks have become less time consuming and more efficient. This has the drawback of having our children believe that we do not need their help. Nothing could be further from the truth. Even if you don't "need" your kids to help out because you are one of those rare women who love to clean, who has a full-time nanny, or who has a regular housecleaner; your kids still need to help! **Keeping house is a basic life skill that every child needs to learn.** Even more important is the fact that a child's healthy self-esteem is linked to how valuable they feel they are. Sticking them in front of a TV or having them play in their room while you (or someone else), does the cleaning is a disservice to your child. This chapter is designed to help you foster their natural desire to help out.

How Moms Train Kids to not Want to do Chores

When it comes to chores, the two messages many Moms send their kids are: "Chores are not fun," and "The household does not need your help." In my family counseling graduate course, Dr. Oscar Christensen said, **"The best thing you can do for a child is to help them believe that the household simply could not run without them." A child who believes this, knows that they are important—knows that they belong.** There are very few children in our technologically advanced nation who hold this belief. On the contrary, they learn that to get out of the way by going out to play is the best way to be helpful. The "go run and play" attitude does not however, establish the sense of contribution that is essential to your child's future well being.

Imagine believing that chores are the most fun thing in the world! What if you believed that chores are more fun than a slumber party with girlfriends, are better than winning a shopping spree at your favorite store, or are more exhilarating than swinging on a swing set under a full moon? Do you think this kind of shift in perspective would motivate you to clean more? Guess what? Your children start out believing that chores are this much fun and more! But most Moms unconsciously destroy this belief. How?

As toddlers, children think chores are an exciting adventure—the vacuum is awe inspiring, dishwashing is possibly as thrilling as baths, and the washing machine is a great appliance that has yet to be discovered. Including young children in the process of chores can be an exhausting experience that can take up to ten times longer than it would take you to do it by yourself. Their ability to perform and complete the chores to your standards will not be up to par, but this is exactly why they need the practice. None of us started out doing anything well. We crawled before we walked and walked before we ran.

Instead of taking the time and patience *[and yes, much is required!]* to teach them how to do chores, we often send our children the message that chores are boring, that chores are "Moms work," and that "going out to play" is a far more desirable choice. But then a funny thing happens. They get older and we suddenly want and *expect* them to help out! But when we ask them to help out we are surprised by their response, "Nope, I'm going out to play." How can this be so surprising when we have been training them for years to do just this?

More often than not, Moms take over when it comes to chores. When you say, "No, no, I'll do it. You're not doing it right," you are subtly telling your child that you don't believe in their ability to learn the task. This is disheartening for and disrespectful of any child. How quickly we forget that we ourselves had to learn each of these tasks bit by bit over time. Taking time for training and making it fun is the key to ensuring your child smiles when doing chores. It does take a lot of time and energy, but once a child sees chores as fun—face it, you've got it made! Ideally, chores should start at the toddler stage, but luckily they can start at any age.

How Little "Princes" and "Princesses" Who Never Lift a Finger Can Turn into Future "Toads"

Many Moms still operate from the old school of parenting where Mom is expected to take on the sole responsibility for the household chores. Allow me to bring you into the 21st Century where Moms have an opportunity to break free from "having" to do all the housework! Times have changed. **A great household runs well when chores and household duties are seen as a team sport and everyone is involved in the game!** Far too often we treat our children like spoiled "Princes" and "Princesses" who are rarely, if ever, expected to lift a finger to help around the house.

Remember the extreme story of my client "Jasmine" in *Chapter One* who dealt with her "Little Prince" of a brother who is now 34 years old? I included this story because the effects of pampering are of increasing concern to me. There are more and more children who are being raised in a pampered fashion. This style of parenting could foretell disaster in the up and coming generation who believe that they are entitled to everything. A generation of "free-loaders" will not take kindly to taking care of you in your old age or taking care of our society. This is preventable and has everything to do with how we are treating and training our children now. All it takes is to give them opportunities to be a contributing player. For those of you with older children, I assure you all is not lost! It may be more work, but it is possible. Make certain you cover the *What Can I do When My Kids Complain or Absolutely Hate Chores?* section.

How to Inspire Children To Get Chores Done

Let's jump right in and start motivating our children to love chores! **Encouragement that inspires your children to do their chores is accomplished by doing the following two things:**

- **Acknowledging**—When a child hears what a difference they are making, you are actively supporting that child's desire to contribute more. A simple, "Thank you so much for clearing the dishes so quickly. It certainly makes my job of loading them easier," or "I so appreciated having you dust today. It makes me feel good when I see the house so clean," can do wonders to encourage your child.

- **Noticing**—This is just a simple form of noticing what your child *has* done. "You did your chores before dinner tonight." "I see that the laundry is all done and put away." "The table is already set I see." Even when the chores are not done perfectly, notice what they did right and make an encouraging observation like, "You really got the bottom sheet on that bed straight today!" "Were you ever thorough when dusting the bookshelf."

Which Chores are Age-Appropriate for My Child?

Often we underestimate just how much a child is capable of doing or being responsible for. The list below outlines age-appropriate chores:

Chores for Preschoolers:

- Put their clothes in the laundry basket.
- Feed the family pet on a daily basis.
- Pull their covers up to make their bed
  [*a few lumps are definitely OK!*].
- Place papers into the recycling box.
- Set the utensils and napkins on the table.
- Put toys away every evening or before their next activity.

Chores for School Aged Children:

- Set the entire table.
- Take out the garbage.
- Recycle.
- Dust.
- Sweep.
- Vacuum.
- Laundry.
- Make their own lunch.
- Help make dinner.
- Load and unload the dishwasher.
- Wash and dry dishes.
- Make their bed.
- Walk the dog.
- Wash the floor.

Chores for Teens:

- Wash the car.
- Wax the floor.
- Buy the groceries.
- Make dinner.
- Buy their clothes and school supplies
  with a budgeted amount of money.
- Mow the lawn.
- Drive younger siblings to school or to events.

Chore Lesson #1: Letting Go of Perfection

It is easy to nit pick when things are not done "The way they should be," or "The way I would have done it." **The ultimate goal of chore training is to encourage teamwork, encourage understanding, and to support our kids in the fashion they deserve—it is not about seeking perfection.** Before you begin to nitpick ask yourself, "Will this matter in a week from now?" The answer to this question can do much to put things in perspective and help you focus on encouraging your children.

Thankfully, letting go of perfection does not mean failing to help children improve upon what they are doing. Nor does it mean accepting work that is done below their capability. The easiest way to figure out if a job has been done well is to ask, "Did my child do their best?" and "Could my child have done better?" If you answer, "yes" to the second question then respectfully point out the improvement required after including feedback on what was done well. For instance, "You made your bed this morning and got the top sheet really straight. All that is needed now are a few tugs and the comforter will lie flat too."

When Your Kids "Forget," Say it Once and then Zip It!

Once you've let go of perfection there may be times when you need to deal with the "I forgot" syndrome. Some days your kids will "forget" to do their chores—they may even refuse. There are two approaches that work equally well:

1. Holding Kids Accountable with Gentle Firmness—

Dr. Jane Nelsen was the first to help me understand how I could easily hold kids accountable to their agreements. This is essential in assisting them to develop responsibility and reliability. If they have agreed to do the dishes right after dinner and instead are listening to the "Top 40 Countdown" on the radio, simply ask: "What was our agreement?" If they laugh, shrug, or look bewildered; ask again, "What was our agreement?" Often their reply will be something like, "I know but they are playing the top five right now and I am dying to hear what they are." Like a broken record, happily ask again; "What was our agreement?" Smile, give your child a hug, and choose not to disagree or argue. Stay with the question—the happier you can be, the better. And just wait! They will come up with all kinds of excuses and suggestions like, "I'll do it tomorrow morning instead." Again, all you need to do is stay quiet, stay happy, and just stay put! The important things to remember here are:

- Ask your child to state the agreement.
- Stay happy.
- Stay put.
- Stay quiet (other than asking about the agreement).

2. Kindly Share Your Needs and Create Guidelines Ahead of Time—In the example of the dishes, you might decide that the dishes need to be washed before having bedtime stories. Clearly state this ahead of time as a fact, not a threat. Simply say, "I know you've agreed to do the dishes before bedtime. Let me know when you're finished and then we can begin stories." Occasionally, when one of the boys had dawdled or "forgotten" to do the dishes we did not have time for bedtime stories. This was not used as a punishment. It was simply following through on the agreement. If your child becomes upset, acknowledge their disappointment and listen to them but remain firm that the dishes need to be done before bed. I often share that, "I too am disappointed that we won't have stories tonight. My guess is that tomorrow night you will do the dishes quickly so we will have lots of story time together."

If your child outright refuses to do the chores add it to the "family meeting" agenda where you can spend time coming up with solutions together.

What Can I Do When My Kids Complain or Absolutely Hate Chores?

Complaining is bound to happen especially if your kids are not used to doing any chores or have done very few up until now! Older children will mistakenly believe that chores are not fun and somehow "beneath them" *[ironically, they never think that chores are "beneath" a Mom!]*. If this is the case, and you have kids that expect you to do the chores for them, be forewarned that you are going to experience resistance before you see improvement.

How to Deal With the Complaints:

1. **Notice What They're Feeling**—"You look frustrated because you don't want to do your chores like you said you would."

2. **Give Them a Chance to Correct You**—They might say, "No I'm angry because all my friends don't have chores."

3. **Again Notice What They are Feeling**—"So you are feeling angry because it seems unfair that you have chores when your friends don't."

4. **Plan a Time to Discuss in the Near Future**—Suggest discussing it at a "family meeting" when they are willing to find a solution that is agreeable to you.

All you need to do is to hear them, not take away their chores. Just hear them. This is definitely easier said than done, since in the heat of the moment all you might want to do is say something like, "You spoiled brat! That isn't true and you know it. All your friends have chores. I am sick and tired of being the only one who does anything around here. Blah, blah, blah, blah, blah!" This tirade might feel good for the moment but it only leaves a child feeling more discouraged. Again, we behave badly when we feel badly; thus, this method will only work if you want to continue experiencing chore conflict.

The more encouraged a child feels, the more fun the child will have. Getting children to feel good about chores requires time. **Giving kids choices when it comes to their chores is an essential aspect of the motivation process.** Many families use a "chore wheel" or "chore jar" that outlines all the chores in the home. Each week everyone chooses their chores or rotates chores. As a family, choose which type of chore schedule your household will follow. Then let the fun begin!

The Art of Making "Chores = Fun" for You and Your Kids

When you talk about chores with your kids it is most helpful when you refrain from groaning and moaning about them yourself. Instead of saying things like, "Aw, I have to do so much around here," use an enthusiastic comment like, "I get to do my chores now!" Granted it may take time to muster up this kind of excitement for chores, especially when you are cleaning the toilet! How can you have fun with chores when you don't like them yourself!? Choose to change your attitude and find ways of making them fun. Since children model what they see, choose to walk your talk and consider using the following suggestions.

Four Ways to Make Chores Fun:

1. **Dance Your Way to Spotless**—Put on your favorite music or your kids' favorite music and dance while you do your chores.
2. **Make it into a Game**—Keep a log that tracks how quickly and thoroughly *[this is important to add!]* your kids can do their chores. Time them and have fun.
3. **Connect with Chores**—Use chore time to catch up on what's important to your kids. Share your day and ask them to share their day.
4. **Story Chores**—Take turns creating a story together. Alternate stringing sentences or words together to create a fun story.

Why Should Kids Not be Paid to Do Their Chores?

To pay or not to pay—that is the question! This is a controversial topic. There is no doubt that paying your kids is a powerful incentive, which will motivate them to get chores done. Some experts claim paying your children for chores will teach your kids what they need to learn about earning money in the "real world." It is a valid point; however, in the "real world" we don't get paid to do our chores unless we are doing chores in someone else's home! **Paying your child is a risky proposition especially if they decide to go on strike or demand higher wages.** Does this mean you don't pay them for anything? If your child is looking to earn extra money, help them find a job outside of the home or pay them for the jobs you would normally pay someone else to do such as: cutting the lawn, raking the leaves, gardening, or washing the car. **The goal of chores is to encourage your child to contribute to the household while receiving the internal satisfaction that comes from a job well done.** We will delve further into the subject of money in *Chapter Fourteen, "Your Kid's Allowance—It's Just Common Cents'"* where I will discuss the most effective use of allowances in great detail. Make certain that you read the diary entry before this chapter as it illustrates the negative impact of paying children for doing their chores.

Which chores will you and your child do this week? If there is a dad or other adult in your household, make certain they complete something from the chore list too and remember to acknowledge them for doing it.

Chapter Tips:

1. Surprise! Children secretly like to do chores!
2. You can help your children to enjoy doing chores by "dancing your way to spotless," making chores into a fun game or using chores as a time to connect.
3. If your children forget their chores, remind them once and then zip it!

Taking Action:

1. Have your children choose a daily chore and brainstorm ways in which you can make that chore over-the-top fun!
2. Notice anything your child does that helps you out during the week and thank them for it.
3. Ask your child to help out: "Would you hold this door open for me please?" "Would you help me carry this?" "Would you do me a favor and bring this to my room?" Make certain your requests are polite and that you thank them for their help.

Dear Diary,

Just received an email from Leanne, an Elementary school teacher, who shared how encouragement transformed a difficult student's life. Here is what she said:

When I first met my student "Steve" he was a bit of a mess. He would roll around on the floor during instructions, hand in work that was incomplete and did not have friends because the other kids thought he was weird. Steve was often in trouble and was in the principal's office a lot. Something needed to be done.

After many meetings we came up with a plan designed to encourage him. At the end of each day, Steve would fill out his "Success Book," where he would write three things that went well for him, and I would tell him one thing I noticed that went well. Each evening, Steve's parents would sign the "Success Book" and write down one thing that had gone well for him at home. All day long, I would notice things that were going well. On the playground, Steve was allowed to take out the basketball and as a result he became a great player! Slowly we began to notice changes—he chose to behave well more often, he was called to the principal's office less and kids began asking if they could play with him on the court at recess.

You would not recognize Steve today. He now walks with his head high. He is kind, caring and has lots of friends. Steve is so pleased. His parents are pleased. The principal is really pleased! We have all witnessed a transformation in Steve's life because of the basic Adlerian principle: encouragement.

Kelly

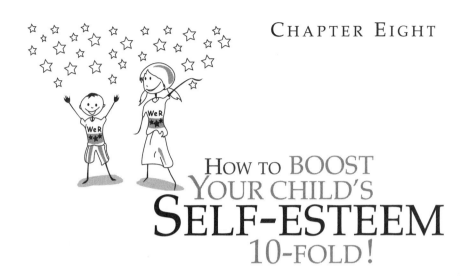

How to BOOST YOUR CHILD'S SELF-ESTEEM 10-FOLD!

How Encouragement Can Save You Thousands of Dollars in Future Therapy

"Screw you Mom!" and the slam of the front office door was all that I heard one Monday morning from one of my new clients. By the time I rounded the corner of the counseling waiting room, I saw five people staring at a middle-aged Mom who was steaming! This was the mother of the sixteen-year-old who had just left the building. The Mom began to rant; "Just has to embarrass me doesn't she! Thinks she knows everything when she knows nothing!" Then her daughter returned, "Oh, I suppose you're going to tell her how horrible I am. Well it takes one to know one MOTHER!"

This was the beginning of my counseling sessions with a sixteen year old who ran away from home on a regular basis, who was sleeping with a twenty-three year old, and who began to cut classes. Making significant changes was near impossible, as her parents refused to come to our counseling sessions and instructed me to "fix her!" Her parents remained oblivious to the damage they were doing with their discouraging "fat cow" comments and other putdowns. Little did they know that by learning how to encourage their daughter when she was a child they would have saved themselves thousands of dollars in time and therapy. They also missed out on learning the tools that could have nurtured their relationship. **It is never too late to repair emotional damage in your family if you are willing to go the distance.** This chapter is intended to give you the tools necessary to keep you and your kids from wasting endless money and energy on therapy to repair a broken relationship which could have been prevented.

The Silent Cries of Your Kids and What They Mean

Why is encouragement so important? Because it can dissolve misbehavior better than anything else! **Rudolph Dreikurs said, "A misbehaving child is a discouraged child."** When children fail to receive encouragement, they look for ways to gain the attention they seek through ineffective means such as: aggression, bullying, disrespect and even coach potato behavior. **By encouraging our children we can prevent the very misbehavior that we don't like.** Doesn't this sound nice!?

Have you ever noticed that when you feel fine your day goes fine? Kids are the same, when they feel well, they tend to do well; when they feel bad, they tend to do bad. **How we feel about who we are has everything to do with how we behave.** When children feel they are not getting enough attention, when they feel that they have lost control and when they feel unimportant they act out. During these moments kids unconsciously believe that misbehaving is the answer to their problem. But it is a "mistaken" solution, which only deepens their discouragement.

Who are Your Models of Encouragement?

Encouragement is an art form that many Moms were neither taught, nor experienced much of, in their childhood. Whether Trivial Pursuit is your game or not, you would probably have difficulty naming all the recipients of the past five Nobel Peace Prizes, naming the five wealthiest people on earth, or naming the best dressed male and female of last year. Yet, if I asked you, "As a child, who encouraged you the most?" "Which teacher inspired you to learn?" "Which person made you feel like one of the most special people on the planet?" You may find that these questions are easier to answer! **What we *do* is not nearly as important as who we *are*. People are not going to remember your child's resumé as much as they will remember how they felt when they were around her.**

People who encouraged you as a child are the models I invite you to focus on now—those people who loved you for you, not for what you did or did not do. Those who saw your gifts, who spent time teaching you, and who encouraged your light to shine brightly; these are the people you most likely wanted to spend time with. You likely cherish these models to this day. Yet, many of us are still under the misconception that a big part of being a Mom is pointing out our child's faults and fixing them.

If you asked the Mother of my client, mentioned at the beginning of this chapter, if she loved her daughter and if she wanted the best for her she would have undoubtedly said, "Yes." This mother believed that the reason for kicking her daughter out of the house, for calling her a "fat pig," and for reading her diary, was because she "loved her and needed to teach her what was right and wrong." Yet, clearly from their interaction, her daughter did not feel loved. Instead of bringing them closer together, the punishments forced them further apart. I don't want you to make the same mistake.

What are True Words of Encouragement?

Encouragement is the best gift you can give your children. Encouragement and praise are often mistakenly believed to be the same thing when they are actually quite different. **Encouragement is a "gift" focusing on the internal process—the "who" our child is. Praise is given as a "reward" for external results—for the "what" our child does.** The easiest way to remember the differences is as follows:

Encouragement—are all the phrases and words you would use during a game or race. Things like:

- "Way to go!"
- "You can do it."
- "Great save."
- "You look like you are really enjoying yourself."

- "Awesome job!"
- "Look at all the effort you are putting in."
- "I bet you were proud of that goal."

Encouragement inspires children to dig deep within themselves to do better, to reach for more, and to achieve their dreams. It is also the building block for intrinsic satisfaction that comes from a job well done or knowing you did your best.

Praise—consists of all the phrases and words you would use once your child's team has won. Examples are as follows:

- "I am so proud of you. You won!"
- "You're a winner. I love you."
- "We're number one, we're number one!"
- "You're first, like your sister."
- "Finally, you won."

Praise focuses on the results of one's efforts. Praise is a form of extrinsic satisfaction that can be highly motivating but addictive.

What Can Make or Break Your Child's Self-Esteem?

When children are fed a diet of praise they begin to rely on "external rewards" to boost their self-worth. The type of motivation creates a never-ending cycle of comparison to highly unattainable standards. This produces children who are "pleasers" and "perfectionists" who are constantly in the rat race struggling to achieve in order to prove their worth. **While most of us like to give and to receive praise, encouragement is what contributes most to our children's self esteem.** How does it do this? **When kids are encouraged they are inspired by the "internal motivation" of doing their best. They learn to enjoy the journey itself, excited to give life their "all!" Encouraged children naturally seek achievement as a way to express who they really are. They have the desire to lend a helping hand and a wish to contribute their unique gifts to the world. It is this attitude of positively driven passion that will take our children far in life.**

Praise is not evil. It *is* ineffective in fostering the internal support—their self-esteem. The more you focus on encouraging phrases and words, the more likely your child is to feel good about who they are. Children who are encouraged strive for their own excellence, rather than the perfection praise fosters. There is already tremendous pressure on our kid's to become the best in all they do. When they don't have that intrinsic core strength of knowing they are a worthwhile person just as they are, they can become obsessed with being perfect. This can lead to anorexia, mononucleosis, depression, or alcohol and drug abuse. **When children feel good about who they are, there is little that can stop them from attaining their dreams!**

Encouraging Phrases that Transform Your Kid's Day!

How would your child's day, week and life be different if you chose to feed them a constant stream of encouragement such as what is found below?

Encouraging Phrases that Transform Your Kid's Day!

- "Look how much you have improved."
- "Way to go!"
- "You must be proud of yourself."
- "Thanks so much for holding the door open for me."
- "I am so blessed to have a child like you in my life."
- "You made such a difference by helping me with dinner."
- "It's obvious that you did your very best."
- "What would you do?"
- "I love you."
- "I really enjoyed laughing with you tonight."
- "I have faith in you."
- "I really enjoyed the time we spent together."
- "I am so proud of who you are becoming."
- "I enjoyed watching you help your brother learn to write."
- "What was your favorite part of the day?"
- "You will make the best decision for you."

- "Tell me more."
- "You're improving your reading each and every day!"
- "What do you like about your picture?"
- "What do you think about that?"
- "How exciting for you!"
- "There is no one I would rather spend time with than you."
- "I like the colors you chose in that painting."
- "I can see you are having an awesome time. "

Do you think hearing the above encouraging phrases day in and day out would make a difference to how your child operates in the world? How did you feel after reading these phrases? Warm and fuzzy all over? Now compare this feeling with what you feel after reading the list of praise phrases below:

- "I am proud of you because you got that A."
- "You won!"
- "You got that goal just like your sister in her first game."
- "If you would add some green then it will be perfect."
- "You are always such a *good* son!"
- "Are you ever the best looking person in your class!"
- "You are the fastest on your team."
- "You always behave well."
- "That's the best picture you have ever done."

How would you feel and what conclusions would you make about yourself and others if you heard praises like those above? You'd want to act in ways that would get you more praise! Hopefully, by now you are starting to see the difference. The praise list above will teach your child to become a "pleaser," a "perfectionist" who strives to be better than others—living life for someone else. The list you want to focus on is the first list—the encouragement list. Why? **Encouragement, moment after moment, is what leads to great things.**

How to be Certain You are Using Encouragement Effectively

Words and phrases are only a small part of encouragement. Encouragement can happen without any words at all. Sometimes a hug, smile, or a fun wink can be just as encouraging as anything you say. Families who have a secret handshake, bedtime ritual, or special tradition are all using powerful forms of encouragement. These actions let your children know just how much you appreciate them even when you are busy on the phone or are caught up in a project that takes you away from giving them 100% of your attention.

It is your tone, intention, and body language that ultimately delivers the message your child hears. You can say "I love you" a million ways. If you say it with a scowl on your face your child can easily translate it to mean, "I hate you." It is therefore essential to check in with yourself. What are your intentions. Ask yourself, "Would I be using this same tone or phrase with a good friend? An acquaintance?" Are you saying something like, "Oh, look you got an 'A,' just like your brother," because you really want them to get more "A's?" While, we'd all love our kids to get "A's," real success comes when our children *want* to get an "A" for themselves, not to please us.

What Graham Wants You to Know About Yelling

One of the most encouraging things we can do is to commit to a "No Yelling Policy." Years ago, the boys were interviewed in one of my family counseling courses at my graduate school. Sitting in the audience, I was amazed to hear Graham's answer to the question, "What do you most like about Kelly?" Immediately, he replied, "She doesn't yell." Months later I asked him, "What advice would you give to parents wanting to improve?" Again he replied, "Don't yell at your kids." He was definitely consistent. It may be easy to forget the times when we have "lost it." Yet, these are the moments our children's hearts may never forget. **Yelling *at* your**

children is not a solution; it is what can create problems. A "No Yelling Policy" gives us time to "catch" ourselves *before* we get carried away and say something we might regret. Choosing to adopt this policy can help us remember to calm down before discussing "heated issues" with our kids. This policy can also prevent both the escalation of disagreements and of hurt feelings. Yet, if you do happen to "loose it" (*after all you are human and have one of the most challenging jobs on earth!*) make certain you perform a "Daring Do Over" as quickly as possible (*described in Chapter Nine*).

How You Can Stop Your Kid from Driving You Crazy

The proactive form of parenting I have been sharing is quite opposite to the "feel bad" philosophy many parents unknowingly use. The method I espouse uses a "feel good" philosophy—supporting our kid's natural desire to do well! We have been taught to use a "feel bad" approach, in which our children pay for their mistakes. This belief system has brought us to where we are today—with stressed out, burnt out Moms who know there has to be a better way of parenting. The "feel good" approach to family problems is paramount in the success of resolving conflict easily and effortlessly. **By encouraging our kids in the midst of conflict we can help to change their negative state of mind, which leads them to act out in the first place!**

When the kids are driving you crazy, using encouragement as a solution is rarely what you would think of doing. However, using encouragement during conflict is one of the best and most effective times to do so. **While we all handle stress differently, encouragement in times of chaos is the most direct route to give us what we most want and need—peace *[sigh]*, understanding *[ah, yes!]*, and cooperation *[hallelujah!]*.** Remember, children who choose to be well behaved tend to be those who feel encouraged. In the heat of the moment, if you encourage your kids by acknowledging their feelings, or by giving them a hug and asking them to help you find a solution, your kids will likely respond positively. Children (like Moms) are going to have "bad hair days." Choosing to encourage them, rather than nag at them, can help transform their day and improve their problem solving skills. **The next** time you notice your children are having a "bad hair day" give them a giant hug, ask them out on a special date, or leave them a banner across their room telling them how wonderful they are!

How to Best Encourage Each of Your Children

There are three easy ways to encourage your children regardless of their interests:

- **Stay Away from Comparisons at all Costs.** Comparing your children can easily slip into conversation. Comments like, "Why can't you just be more like your brother?" are damaging. Watch your intentions. Are you trying to get your child to be something that they are not? Remember the most encouraging thing you can do for them is focus on their strengths rather than their weaknesses.

- **Provide Opportunities for Your Family to Function as a Team.** Implementing "family meetings" *[as outlined in Chapter Five]* will go a long way in establishing support for each child. Using heart-felt communication exercises and forming your own rituals will further a feeling of contribution, belonging, and inner satisfaction.

- **Never Leave the Eldest Child "In Charge" of the Younger Ones.** The only circumstance where an eldest child should be left to "take care of" the younger children is when there is a huge gap in age (at least five years or more) and the younger children are babies or toddlers. Telling the younger children that they need to listen to everything their older brother or sister says supports a hierarchical system and promotes competition. This approach encourages eldest children to become "bossy" and when this happens younger children will rebel in their own way. Instead, make it clear that everyone is in charge of themselves. Discuss your expectations while you are away and let them know that you have faith in all of them.

The 10 Top Ways to Encourage Your Children Today:

Mystery solved! After reading this chapter, I trust you realize that the main reason your kids misbehave is because they want to be encouraged *[the same applies to your spouse by the way!]*. Here are 10 simple ways to encourage your children today:

1. Smile and "light up" when they come into the room.
2. Focus on their strengths rather than on their weaknesses.
3. Every night say to them, "I am so blessed to have a daughter/son like you in my life."
4. Ask them for their opinion on an issue you have.
5. "Catch them" doing things you love and acknowledge them for it.
6. Become interested in what they are passionate about by asking questions and learning more.
7. Hug them often.
8. Look for ways they can help out and thank them for it.
9. Place surprise notes of encouragement in their lunch or under their pillow.
10. Use encouraging phrases like, "You must be proud of yourself."

Chapter Tips:

1. Dr. Rudolph Dreikurs said, "A misbehaving child is a discouraged child" therefore, one of the best cures for misbehavior is encouragement.

2. True encouragement means focusing on *who* your children are rather than on *what* they do.

3. When your kids are having a "bad hair day" sometimes all they need is a good long hug.

Taking Action:

1. Choose one of the top 10 ways to encourage your child and commit to doing it today. Write down what you will do to encourage your child here:

    _____

    _____

2. Go out of your way to notice what you like about others and share it with your child.

3. Choose to leave the room or calmly state what you are feeling rather than yelling things at your child that you will later regret.

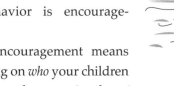

Dear Diary,

Today I caught myself in the act of teaching Grant to lie
to me! He had his friend "James" over and they wanted a
Coke. As they already had treats I told them, "You may
have a Coke tomorrow." Minutes later they had a new angle,
"May we go to the store?" Knowing that they would just
buy a Coke, I denied their request, "You may go to the store
tomorrow." Stubborn, they returned with, "May we go to the
park?" Now the park is not far from the store and my "gut"
told me that they were using the park as an excuse to go
past the store. Just before I said "no", I stopped!

I had a choice: was a Coke worth having Grant lie to me?
No. Grant will be a teenager soon and the last thing I want
is for him to start lying to me about things like alcohol,
drugs, or sex. So I said: "Grant, you are capable of making decisions about your health. Being a 'health nut' I do
my best to provide nutritious meals. However, when you are
out with friends you will need to make up your own mind.
I don't want you to ever feel you need to hide what you are
doing. If you want to go to the store, go." Grant replied,
"Now I feel bad. Maybe we shouldn't go."

Sometimes that reverse psychology stuff really works! But
instead of using it to my advantage, I said, "If you choose
to go, enjoy it!" He ended up going. When they returned
Grant proudly said, "I made a healthy choice. Instead of
Coke, I chose a Coke Slurpee because it has more water in it
and that's healthy!" Well, at least he's thinking about health
but more importantly, he's being honest!

Kelly

CHAPTER NINE

How to
KEEP YOUR
SANITY IN TIMES
OF CONFLICT

Are You Encouraging Your Kids to Lie?

The journal entry opening this chapter illustrates a moment when I realized I was teaching Grant to lie to me. When Moms lay down the law with little, or no flexibility, they unknowingly motivate their children to choose the path of least resistance—they lie! Kids, like adults, want their way. If what you are saying doesn't seem genuinely fair to them they just might begin to lie. A nightmare for every parent includes:

- Getting a call from the Police telling you that your kid has been drinking and driving when you thought he was just sleeping over at a friend's house.

- Finding out that your daughter is pregnant after she swears she has "only kissed" her boyfriend.

- Being told your child is taking drugs when you didn't even think he had ever smoked a cigarette!

The most encouraging part of these worst-case scenarios is that they are, for the most part, preventable. **Establishing open communication with your kids now will increase the likelihood of this honesty being intact during the crucial teen years.** Did you ever lie to your parents? Do you think your kids might be inclined to do the same? As straight and narrow as I was as a teen, I used the occasional "white lie" *[like telling my dad I was going up to bed and instead jumping over the balcony to hang out with my friends!]*. Somehow I seemed perfectly justified in doing what I did. To this day my dad doesn't know about my "white lies" *[Well, at least until now! GULP!]*.

109

How about you? Were there any lies that you told your parents? What about recent ones? There are many adult women who still lie about their job, relationships and family life when it comes to their parents. It starts early on! This chapter will give you the tools that will decrease the amount of time spent in the "deep end"—inspiring greater honesty in your home.

How to Choose Your Fights Wisely so You Don't All Lose

The first major challenge when it comes to conflicts is that we are taught to win! And if there is a winner, there will always be a loser. The last thing we want is for our kids to feel like "losers." When we are fighting with our kids we may be fighting about things that are really none of our business—like the Coke scenario in the diary section. **An important aspect of staying out of the "deep end" is not going there in the first place. Realize that you don't always need to restrict, engage, or comment. Imagine that!**

Many times Moms get involved even though they don't need to! This is good news, because not getting involved may just free up some of your precious time. When it comes to certain issues it is simply not worth the fight. Pick your fights wisely! Dr. Gary McKay and Dr. Dinkmeyer in their book *STEP* developed a simple way to determine whether or not to get involved in an issue. Ask yourself these three questions:

1. Are my basic rights being disrespected?
2. Is someone getting hurt?
3. Are someone's material items in danger of being destroyed?

If you answer "yes" to any of the above, then by all means get involved. But if you answer "no," all you need to do is to support your children in making the best decision for themselves. Often this means saying nothing at all!

How Thinking Before You Act
Can Save You from Many Regrets

When Moms are stressed, words can fly out of their mouths that would put Madam Medusa to shame: "You are just like your Father!"

"How can you be so selfish?" "You're a screw up and you know it." These are the words of an exploding mother who speaks before she thinks and then later regrets what she has said. Most mothers can recall a couple of times when they said something that they later wished they could take back *[maybe they even wished they could wash their own mouth out with soap!]*. When this happens we are caught up in reacting rather than responding. When our emotions are on automatic pilot we use a fight or flight response. This type of trigger occurs in what best-selling author Jane Nelsen calls the "reptilian brain." And Jane often points to the fact that reptiles eat their young!

Cannibalism notwithstanding, if each of us had our own parenting coach who followed us around guiding us, *[and making certain we were getting enough sleep!]*, we may rarely (if ever) experience "ugly" moments. Luckily, there are constructive things we can do on our own to deal with frustration so we don't end up taking it out on our kids. The next three sections: 1) taking a "Mom Time-Out," 2) doing the unexpected, and 3) asking your kids for help, provide many useful frustration-saving tips and techniques.

"Time-Out" Secrets: for You and the Kids

Parents and teachers worldwide have used "time-outs" as a form of punishment. If you are one of the millions who have used the technique you may have been either pleasantly surprised or sorely disappointed. Here is what happened when I first tried this technique. One afternoon, I had a screaming seven year old on my hands who refused to go on a "time-out" so I decided it was my duty to "make him." I carried him kicking and screaming to his room. This only resulted in bruises, a slammed bedroom door, and me laughing at him. Yes I did do this! My laughing then caused him more anger resulting in screaming, fussing, and name-calling. Needless to say this "time-out" experience was not useful. It is important to note that traditional "time-outs" tend to work better with toddlers *[children tend to talk back more, are heavier and may call your bluff!]*. *There is* however, an approach to "time-outs" that can be even more effective.

The only kind of "time-outs" that actually work all the time, every time, are what I call a "Mom's Time-out!" This is where Mom takes the "time-out!" **It is always easier to control what *you* do, rather than what your child does. A** "Mom's Time-Out" is a short period of time that gives you the break you need to deal with the situation effectively. It has the sole purpose of helping you calm down in order to find a positive solution to the problem. It can be a short walk, a minute of deep breathing or just sitting on your "throne" *(otherwise known as the toilet).* Taking a "time-out" also provides a model for your kids to follow when they are faced with their own challenges. Taking time to self-soothe, to calm down, and feel better is a learned skill useful for effectively dealing with conflict. It also ensures that you don't react from that reptilian brain we spoke of earlier—eating your child alive!

"But what if my child is young and can't be left alone?" Excellent question. "What if they follow me while I am on a 'Mom's Time-Out'?" Another good question. Here is the good news: a "Mom's Time-Out" although a little more difficult, can be taken while you are in the same room with your kids. It is a time when you completely disengage in order to recharge your own batteries. A "Mom's Time-Out" gives you the opportunity to return to a place of love and to find the desire to seek a solution rather than to have the desire to give your child a million lashes with a wet noodle!

The Best Way to Use a "Mom's Time-Out!"

1. **Identify Your Feeling and State that You are Taking a "Mom's Time-Out."** Take responsibility for your own feelings by using "I—Statements" instead of "You—Statements." Acknowledge what you are feeling in the moment without blaming your child for making you feel that way (e.g. "I am feeling frustrated right now and am going to take a 'time-out.'").

2. **Be Specific About the Time Needed and State Your Ultimate Goal.** Make certain that your goal reflects the desire to bring you and your child closer together (e.g. "I'm going to take a five minute "time-out" so I can feel better and then we can

find a way to enjoy making dinner together. I will speak with you after my 'time-out.'").

3. **Take Your "Time-Out".** Do whatever it is that will help you to feel better. Even if you are in the same room as your child do not fall into the trap of discussing or justifying your "time-out"—keep quiet. Even if your child is standing on their head with their tongue out, teetering on the edge of the table, or giving you every reason in the book as to why you are a horrible Mom—do not say a thing! Talking with your child during "time-outs" disrespects you and teaches them that they cannot trust your word!

4. **Keep Your Promise by Returning in the Stated Time**—Even if you feel like running away from home forever, return in the time stated. If you feel you need more time, tell them (e.g. "I am not feeling better yet and am going to take another five minutes."). Make certain you are not using "time-outs" as punishments but only for the purpose for which they are intended—to feel better in order to be closer.

5. **Discuss the Situation and Involve Your Kids in Finding a Solution!** Thank them for understanding, focus on specific observations, and ask for help (e.g. "Thanks for being patient while I was having my 'Mom's Time-Out.' I was feeling frustrated when you turned your music up after I asked you not to. My goal is to find a way where we can both enjoy dinner together. Would you be willing to help me out? Any ideas how we can do that?"). If your child says he or she doesn't know, invite him or her to share their suggestions later. Share your suggestions. This is also an ideal time to ask what your child was feeling at that moment. Sometimes the solution rests in listening to the feelings of your child. Surprise! Misbehavior can actually mask the pain children are feeling and are not expressing. If the misbehavior starts up again, it is time to put this concern on the "family meeting" agenda to discuss on another day when you and your child are not so stressed.

You may find that your child will start to want to use "time-outs" themselves—they may want to take a "Kid's Time-Out." If they make this decision on their own they are starting to take responsibility for making themselves feel better. Encourage this behavior especially after you see how helpful it is for you! Brainstorm things your child can do during their "Kid's Time-Out" after trying a "Mom's Time-Out" yourself.

Why You'll Want to Honor Your Nasty Negative Feelings

Even when you pick your fights wisely and use "Mom's Time-Outs" there may still be those days "when you are about to go off the deep end." It was Einstein who said, "Chaos is doing the same thing over and over again and expecting a different result." If you are "going off the deep end" on a regular basis, I encourage you to use what has already been suggested and keep on reading.

Negative feelings can be useful for a Mom's growth. Why? **Your "yucky feelings" can be the warning lights on your dashboard of life that alert you to the fact that something needs to change.** This change does not mean that separate living arrangements are required [*asking a child to leave home early, although tempting, is never an encouraging option!*] Often the only change needed is to your beliefs. To change your beliefs you need to acknowledge your feelings so you can deal with the real problem—the beliefs that caused those feelings.

Experiencing negative feelings can be helpful when they motivate you to transform the beliefs that got you into trouble in the first place. Some of these beliefs can cause a "bad-hair day" to go on for years! Let's pretend you hold the belief that "Great Moms do not leave their kids wanting for anything." Do you think this might create some negative feelings? How about when your child forgets to tell you that she needs a costume for school tomorrow? And it's 9 o'clock at night and you're stressed wondering how to pull it off! What if your child forgets to pack his lunch [*after you have reminded him a gazillion times!*] and calls you out of a meeting expecting you to bring it to school? Negative feelings can surface quickly in these circumstances. But if you believe, "Great Moms support, encourage and let their children learn from their own mistakes," little hiccups like these would not cause you grief. Empowered with this belief you can support your child by listening to them and by helping *them* find a solution. You would not choose to make a costume into the wee hours of the night, nor would you drive like a mad woman to deliver a missing lunch. You would save yourself the time, resentment and frustration that would typically accompany this kind of "Mom rescuing." The best part of all is that you would be supporting your child to recover from their own mistakes.

Below is a list of typical "mom-ming" beliefs that lead to positive and negative feelings. Can you see yourself in any of these?

Beliefs That Lead to Negative Feelings	Beliefs That Lead to Positive Feelings
- My kids "make" me crazy!	- I am responsible for my own feelings.
- "Good Moms" fulfill their kids' needs.	- Supportive Moms help their kids to fulfill their own needs.
- I don't have a choice	- I always have a choice any time I choose.
- "Good Moms" never make their kids unhappy or upset.	- When my kids are unhappy my role is to hear them and support them—not necessarily give them what they want.
- I need to show my kids the right way.	- There is more than one way to do something—I am open to learning.
- I need to be in control of my kids.	- Ultimately, I can only control what I do.

Living by the positive beliefs on the right-hand side can radically reduce your "deep end" moments. Consider writing out a list of positive beliefs.

Focus on these helpful affirmations by keeping them in a place where you will see them on a regular basis.

Using "Distraction Actions!"

Instead of doing the expected, it is time to do the unexpected! **When we do the unexpected we can derail a conflict headed for disaster.** Your kids are accustomed to your responses and respond accordingly! Using a "Mom Time-Out" or doing something I call "Distraction Actions" will break the patterns that keep you stuck in conflict! "Distraction Actions" are conscious behaviors used to momentarily distract us from the present conflict. This helps to alter your state of mind, which can diffuse the intensity of the conflict. If you feel frustrated you could react with a "Distraction Action" such as doing 25 jumping jacks while yelling, "We are the greatest family in the world!" Don't be surprised if your child looks at you with a, "Why is Mom acting so weird!?" look. While the jumping jacks may seem silly, could it be an improvement over what is going on now?

"Distraction Actions" are even more powerful when you directly involve your child. For instance you could suggest something like, "Let's see how fast we can run up the stairs while holding hands," or ask, "Would you give me the biggest hug you can possibly give?" or "How loud and then how quiet can we say 'I love you' to each other?" These types of requests can begin to mend the emotional distance created by conflict. **"Distraction Actions" are not the time for pride or humility—it is about looking for ways that can catapult you into shifting perspectives in order to become closer to your children.**

Asking Your Kids for Help in the Heat of the Moment!

In the heat of the moment, when you are looking up at the sky in exasperation and are sending out a silent SOS, ask for help from the very person that may be driving you crazy—your child. **When kids act up they often just need to be involved.** Give them the opportunity. While eating dinner at a family gathering, my young niece (then age six) was acting up and everyone was getting mildly irritated. I looked at her and said, "Would you help me out?" She looked surprised and then flattered, "Would you go into the kitchen and help Grandma bring out the buns and butter." With a smile on her face she got busy and forgot all about misbehaving. **We all want to be helpful—sometimes shifting your children's mental state is just a matter of giving them an opportunity to feel useful.**

Guilt Free "Daring Do Overs!"

At some time Moms will "lose it" and wish that they could take a comment back. Good news! Now you can by using a "Daring Do Over." "Daring Do Overs" happen when we dare to realize we made a mistake and ask to do it over—to practice doing it well. This exercise is like the rewind button for your life—your "take two" opportunity in which you can do it all over again.

A "Daring Do Over" Does Three Things:

1. It shows your child that it is important to you to make it better.
2. It retrains your mind and establishes new healthy habits.
3. It models for your child that we can learn from our mistakes and correct them.

Kids love "Daring Do Overs!" It is like playing a game in which they can help you out for a change! **So the next time you do something in which you think, "Oh I could have done that one better," ask for a "Daring Do Over" where you just do better, rather than feel guilty.**

Apologies: When to Ask and When to Give

When we do wrong to another, apologies can be the path to healing. Apologies are precious commodities that are not to be thrown around lightly in conversation nor wasted during a heated discussion. In times of conflict we may say something like, "I expect an apology young lady!" in a tone that means "NOW!" This is a type of punishment and is not useful to anyone. The time for apologies is when all parties have calmed down enough to hear and feel them.

Moms absolutely can ask for an apology but for the apology to be effective it needs to have flexible terms. A request for an apology should sound like, "I would like an apology when you are ready to give one." This statement is honest, respectful, and clear. Moms aren't the only ones deserving of an apology: it is important for Moms to apologize too! Some parents believe that parents don't have to apologize, yet apologies can mean so much to our kids. Anyone who has given an apology to a child knows that the automatic response is, "That's OK." Children have an awesome knack of letting things go. We would all do well to learn from their ability to forgive and make up.

Chapter Tips:

1. The only person in this world you can truly change is YOU!

2. Your "yucky feelings" are telling you that something needs to change.

3. When you are in the "deep end," having the courage to take a "Mom's Time-Out" and then inviting your children to help you find a solution can actually bring you closer together.

Taking Action:

1. Practice one "Mom's Time-Out" this week. When you take your "time-out" make certain that you do not speak to your child. **Let us know how it goes by sharing your stories at: www.ultimateparenting.com.** ☺

2. If you do something you regret, instead of beating yourself up, ask your child for a "Daring Do Over" and practice, practice, practice!

3. Choose a "Distraction Action" that you would be comfortable using. The crazier— the more effective it tends to be!

    "Distraction Actions" I might use are:

    _____

    _____

    _____

    _____

    _____

    _____

Dear Diary,

Yesterday morning, I decided to do something about Grant's dawdling since Graham is often late for school as a result! So I told the boys that I would leave at 8 am sharp. 7:52 am came and they were both rushing around. 7:55 Graham is getting his coat on. 7:58 Graham is out the door waiting. No Grant. I had made myself a promise to follow through.

When my watch turned 8 am I took a big gulp and left with Graham as Grant screamed from the front door: "GET BACK HERE! I'M READY TO GO! COME BACK!!!" Graham was delighted with his special time with me. But I was freaking out! Even though Grant was of age, all I could think about was what I would say to the cops if Grant called them like he had threatened. I saw the headline: CAREGIVER NEGLECTS BLIND CHILD, SENTENCED TO 6 MONTHS IN PRISON.

Relieved, I returned to the house without a police car in sight. I opened the door to find Grant sitting in a heap no more ready than he was at 8 am. I told him, "When you are all ready to leave, let me know and I would be happy to take you." That's when the debate started: "You didn't help me find my homework! My watch said 7:55 am" I wanted to lash back, but I didn't. Instead I pulled out something much more powerful—the vacuum. And vacuum I did with a couple, "Sorry Grant I can't hear you. When you're ready to go let me know." It wasn't until 10:45 am that he was ready. The motivation? He realized he was missing recess! We did have a good time walking to school. But the best part—today he was on time!

Kelly

HOW TO GIVE
YOUR CHILD CHOICES
THAT WON'T
HAUNT
YOU LATER

The Damaging Effects of Growing Up with Little Choices

The good news is that you are one of the most influential people in your kid's life. The bad news is that you are one of the most influential people in your kid's life. How you impact your children is directly related to how you choose to parent. I have met many parents *[especially fathers]*, who mistakenly believe that they are in control. Yet, when their kids rebel or begin to follow another leader they are surprised. **If we fail to teach children to think for themselves and learn from their mistakes we are setting up future heartache.** Parents who have strict household rules fail to realize that they are not effectively preparing their kids for a world in which there is increasingly more decisions to be made.

As a teen, I witnessed the effects of a controlling father in a friend of mine named "Jan." I enjoyed Jan's humor but noticed that she would become quiet when she brought up her father. A couple of sleepovers later and I found out why. Jan's father decided what food she ate, what clothes she wore and what courses she took. When she came out with my family for dinner at a restaurant one night, we marveled at how painful it was for her to decide what she wanted to eat off the menu. She struggled until she gave up and chose the same entrée as I did. The sad part of this story is that we did not remain friends for long. She soon found a new crowd to hang out with and when they offered her drugs she just went with the crowd.

Jan's dad believed his authoritarian approach was in her best interest. He thought he was protecting her, but instead he was handicapping her with a home devoid of choices. This prevented her from developing her decision-making abilities; the very thing that I believe led her to take drugs. **If we do not give our children the opportunity to make choices and to experience the effects of their choices, we are doing them a grave disservice that can literally cost them their lives.**

Since You Will Never be in Control of Your Kids What's Your Best Bet?

Despite the billions of choices you will be given in your lifetime, it will not include the choice of controlling your children. If you haven't figured this one out yet, you are in for a rude awakening. **Whether you believe it or not you will never be in complete control of your kids. Never. Nada. Not a chance.** Coming to grips with this realization opens the door for an alternative approach—an approach that utilizes choices.

Why choices? Because giving your child choices like: "What would you like for a vegetable tonight—peas or carrots?" "Which shirt do you want to wear—blue or yellow?" will train your kids in the art of decision-making—one of the most important skills you can give to your child. **Making choices is key to the outcome of a child's life. Wise decisions in the future only come from experiencing the consequences of making a choice today.** When children are not given the opportunity to make their own decisions they can be emotionally crippled for life. They can grow into adults who do not know what makes them happy, not know what their purpose is, and not know what they want to do in life.

Choices allow our children to make the following decisions:
- To decide whether or not to take drugs.
- To stand up for themselves.
- To walk away from violence.
- To choose friends who support them.
- To end friendships that are unhealthy.
- To pick high school courses that they are interested in.

- To decide if, and when, to have sexual intercourse.

The above choices are essential decisions that our children will eventually face no matter how old they are now.

Why Believing that We Always Have a Choice in Every Situation Can Positively Change You and Your Kid's Life

Do any of the following sound familiar?

- Friends have asked you to come over for dinner and you say "yes" even though your week is packed and all you feel like doing is going home.
- Someone asks for help and even though you don't have time you say, "yes."
- An acquaintance you don't like has cornered you in the grocery store and you politely listen for over 15 minutes.

Situations like the ones above can leave us filled with frustration, depression, and exhaustion. If you have ever said, "I have to..." you are one of the millions of women (including me) who sometimes believe that you don't have any other choice. When we feel "stuck" in a job just to pay the rent, "stuck" in a relationship because there might be nothing better, or "stuck" making lunches because "that's just what Moms do"—you may feel like you don't have a choice. But wait a minute! Sometimes we don't have a choice! If this thought just went through your mind then you are fooling yourself. **It is a mistaken belief that we sometimes do not have a choice. Even when we cannot change another person or a situation, we can always change how we feel.** The answer to getting "unstuck" rests in realizing this very truth: we always have a choice.

We can choose differently whenever we don't like a situation. Even prisoners have a choice and have found liberation by choosing to escape their painful circumstances through their imagination. **When we recognize that we always have a choice, we open the door to endless possibility.**

Far too often, women stay in unhealthy jobs, unhealthy relationships, and unhealthy situations even though they are not happy. They fool themselves into believing that they don't have a choice. Coming clean by saying, "I choose to stay in an unhealthy job because I am scared to be without a paycheck," is a big step forward. When we take responsibility for our choices and help our kids to do the same, we begin to see a world of possibility rather than a world of unchanging absolutes in which we play the victim. Victims believe that they don't have a choice and give up on life; living someone else's dream.

Are You "Shoulding" All Over Your Self?

Much of our language actually supports a victim mentality. **On a subconscious level these words only keep us stuck in our old ways. Words like:**

Should	*vs.*	*Like to/Love to*
Have to	*vs.*	*Get to*
Must	*vs.*	*Want to*
Need to	*vs.*	*Choosing to*
Can't	*vs.*	*Choosing not to*

It may appear "anal" but the more we use the phrases from the right hand column the more we consciously support an abundant life of opportunities and teach our children to do the same. Choosing to change our language is something that can radically shift our perspective. Using positive language can lead us to make choices that come from our heart.

How to Give Choices Without Causing Chaos!

As awesome as our choices are they are only effective when there are limits. If there are no boundaries your children will begin to call the shots and run wild! **Choices with boundaries prevent chaos.** One thing I regret with Grant and Graham is not using firmer boundaries when it came to food. Instead of keeping the options simple like: "Do you want pasta or soup tonight?" I would instead ask, "What do you want for dinner?" This contributed to Grant becoming a picky eater and to my frustration in trying to accommodate by preparing two meals *[when I only needed to make one!]*. So let me show you how I would offer a dinner option today:

- **Give Your Child an Option**—"Grant, would you like salad or peas tonight?" If he answers with one of the options your job is done. If he says "neither" go to step two.
- **Clarify the Option**—"Neither was not an option. Do you want salad or peas?" If he repeats, "Neither!" go to step three.
- **Give Another Option**—"Would you like to choose or do you want me to choose for you?" The child can then make a decision or may want you to decide. If he says, "I don't know," go to step four.
- **Give a Time Limit**—"I need to know in the next two minutes so I can start dinner. If I do not receive your decision by then I will decide for you. It's your choice."
- **Follow Through**—If they choose not to give you an answer within the two minutes, then they have made their decision— you get to choose.

The above is a simplified version that has potential for all kinds of possible reactions. The key is to remain kind when giving your child options. If you are following each step but are using a tone that says, "Decide or I'm going to really be mad!" the choices you give will be completely ineffective. When starting to use choices do not be surprised if your child is not happy about it. This new strategy requires that your child change. Your child may test you to make certain the change you are implementing is real. If your child has a temper tantrum or becomes angry with you, use your listening skills to validate his feelings. At this point you can say, "You are feeling frustrated because you don't like the choices you have right now. Would you like a hug?" If he doesn't want a hug, tell him, "I can see you are upset and don't want a hug. If you decide that you want one, come find me and I will be happy to give you one."

How to Set Effective Boundaries While Still Liking You:

All kids need boundaries—want boundaries. Boundaries provide comfort, since they allow for an understanding of what is to be expected. Boundaries require that Moms:

1. **Set Clear Parameters**—Be specific and clear: "Do you want one bunch of grapes or two?" or "Are you going to take Drama or Spanish as an elective this year?"

2. **Keep it Simple**—Moms explain things *way* more than they need to. Keep it short and sweet, "Do you want to come with me or stay home with dad?"

3. **Follow Through**—Do what you say you are going to do. Don't change your children's options after they have made their decision.

4. **Respect the Decision They Make**—Sometimes our kids will make decisions we don't agree with or that we know won't have a positive outcome. We may want to say, "I told you so!" The consequences of our children's decisions are part of the learning process. Any negative reaction will teach your children that learning is not fun and that making choices leads to punishment. Support your children and help them to realize that next time they can choose differently: "I see that you didn't have a good time shopping with me, maybe next time you will choose to stay at home with dad."

5. **Be Gentle with Yourself**—Your children aren't always going to like you. The key is to continue loving them and loving yourself even when they don't appear to love you back. Stick with your decision especially when they question you. It may get worse before it gets better. If you have been acting one way for so long, your kids will test your new approach *[you can count on it!]*.

Choices Made Simple at Any Age

Choices can be very simple! They will become more complex as your children are ready for more responsibility. Below I have included word-for-word some choices that you can give your kids.

Choices for Toddlers Need to be Simple:
- "Would you like to wear the blue or green pants today?"
- "Would you like to put away your teddy bear or your video?"
- "Would you like to get into that chair by yourself or with Mommy's help?"

Choices for School Aged Children:
- "Which chore have you chosen this week?"
- "Would you like to help me prepare tonight's dinner or tomorrow's?"
- "What story would you like to hear tonight?"
- "Do you want to complete your homework before snack or after snack?"
- "Which activity would you like to do this season: karate or pottery?"
- "What are the three most important things you want to do this summer?"

Choices for Teens:
- "What day are you going to do the grocery shopping on this week?"
- "I've written a check out for this season's clothing allowance. Would you like to shop alone or would you like me to come along?"
- "You have $250 for activities this semester. Which will you choose?"

By the time they are teens you want them to be making major decisions that include: how to spend their clothing allowance, what courses to take and assisting with household decisions like summer vacations.

How to Say "Yes" and Get What You Want!

We have a choice whether to focus upon what is wrong or on what is right. "NO!" is a word that focuses on the problem rather than on the solution. Although, the word "no" can be powerful, it loses its power when our kids have heard it thousands of times. Many Moms have children who simply no longer respond to the word "No!" [or take minutes to do so]. **Choosing to be more positive can have a huge effect on the entire atmosphere of your household.** One of my favorite tools is saying "Yes" more often even when what I want to say is a flat out "No!" There is an effective way to use "yes" while still getting what you want.

How do you transform your "No" to "Yes?" Easy! Each time you feel yourself wanting to say "No," ask yourself, "When could I say yes to this request?" You might want to use these examples to help create your own answer::

- "Yes, we can have pizza tomorrow night." vs. "No you can't have pizza."
- "Yes, you can go to Cheryl's house on the weekend." vs. "No you can't go to Cheryl's house today."
- "Yes, you can stay up in your room until 1 a.m." vs. "No you can't stay out until 1 a.m."

Your kids will catch on quickly and might say, "I want to have it now!" Simply repeat what you said before. Getting into a discussion will only defeat the purpose.

Another quick tool in terms of saying "Yes!" instead of "No!" is using a decoy approach. This works particularly well for young children. If they are moving towards something that is dangerous or that you don't want them to touch, create a decoy! Instead of yelling, "No!" [This only tells them that there is something obviously exciting to discover!], cry out, "Oh, look at this!" and look the other way. Nine times out of ten they will follow you, curious about what you find so exciting. As they walk over to you encourage them with "Yes, come on over and see this!" Now your job is to make whatever you are looking at exciting, "Oh, wow look at how the hinge doors open and close. Oh, look at the color of this screw!" **Choosing to direct our attention to the positive is a choice that can transform many ugly situations into beautiful moments.**

1-2-3-Poof: Preventing Misbehavior

When it comes to choices we also have the choice to bring more magic into our kids lives. Just like the magic of Disneyland, Moms have the choice of using "Ultimate Mom" magic that can add pixie dust to any regular day. Disney has created a billion dollar industry feeding our creative imagination with magical characters and stories. These stories speak right to the heart of children and can transform a moment from ordinary to extraordinary. **Kids whose creative juices are flowing—who are being entertained, rarely misbehave. Why? Because they are having fun!** They don't have to act out to get attention or to bring excitement to a boring moment. Hundreds of thousands of Mom's know the power of this form of entertainment and actively build a library of videos for this very purpose. Yet, Moms can also use their own misbehaving Mom magic to secure similar results.

Appealing to children's imagination can prevent misbehavior from even starting. Use sentences such as: "Wow, would you look at that!" "Do you want to know a secret?" "Follow me. I've got something weird to show you." This approach requires that you see the world from the perspective of a child—forever fresh. One way of getting into a "playful spirit" is by pretending you are an alien from a different planet where everything is new. How would an alien visitor to this planet think and feel? What would they find interesting?

Making things into a game is another sure way of getting your needs met while also fulfilling your kids' needs. This is a winning recipe for success! "How fast can you clean this up so there are no crumbs left?" is one sure way of having children enjoy the process of cleaning. Does it have to be a game every time—of course not—but you definitely increase the odds of them doing things when they are having a blast! Imagine if you knew that your work was like play—like the best party you have ever been to. Do you think that you might be more motivated to show up? Do you think it might be useful to look at life like this? This is the choice you have. When are you going to play with your kids next?

Chapter Tips:

1. Your child's ability to make wise decisions is only a result of having been given choices and having been given the opportunity to learn from choices made.
2. You always have a choice as to how you respond even when it doesn't feel like you do!
3. The most effective choices must include boundaries.

Taking Action:

1. Write "I don't like _____ but I am choosing to do so because _____." e.g. I don't like getting up at 6 a.m. but I am choosing to do so because I want to have time with my kids. Write down as many choices as you can think of. This is the first step toward taking responsibility for your life. Way to go!

_____

_____

_____

_____

_____

_____

_____

_____

_____

2.   Write down one specific choice that you are committed to giving to your child today. Now go for it!

_____

_____

_____

3.   Do something today that brings some of the Disney magic into your life. Rent a fun movie, buy glitter dust or pretend to be a "hug monster" and hug each of your family members at least eight times today. How I will bring more magic into my family's life:

_____

_____

_____

_____

_____

_____

_____

_____

_____

_____

_____

_____

_____

Dear Diary,

The proactive parenting material works again! Meredith from my parenting class just sent me the following email that I have cut and pasted into my inspiration file:

Kelly, It's a miracle ... only two weeks after your course and I am no longer dealing with my two girls fighting in the car! I was really skeptical when you suggested I tell them that if they "choose" to fight I would pull over and wait in the car until they both told me and showed me they were ready. I did as you said and started it on a day when I had lots of extra time and wham-o they started to fight. So I pulled over just like you said without saying anything (which was the hard part) and began to read my book. It took the girls a couple of minutes to even realize we had stopped! Then it got very quiet and then they started to laugh. Finally, ten minutes later they both told me they were ready to go and I started without saying a thing. It was so much easier than I thought and I was proud that I pulled it off. I've only had to use it two more times since and I actually find myself wishing they would take longer so I would have more reading time!

How can I thank you except to say ... THANK YOU, THANK YOU, THANK YOU!

Sincerely,

Meredith—Mother Who Gets Pushed Around in the Car No More!

CONSEQUENCES THAT SAVE A MOM TIME AND FRUSTRATION

The Good, Bad, and Ugly of Rewarding Behavior!

Rewarding behavior with stickers, candy, and money is a common occurrence. It is tempting to use rewards as they can be extraordinarily effective in coercing a child to do what we want. Some psychologists refer to this method as "positive reinforcement" or "behavior modification." And it will work—no doubt about it. Yet, it has one major pitfall that many Moms do not foresee.

Children whose sole reason for good behavior is to "get" a reward will eventually find that not all behavior is externally rewarded. A "what's in it for me" mentality does not support true self-esteem in which children genuinely seek to contribute positively to others. Problems can occur when kids learn to use rewards as a bargaining tool by saying things like, "I will only do _____ if you do this." And their demands can become expensive the older they get! Suddenly chocolate bars in grade school become the latest and greatest designer clothes or computer equipment in their tweens and teens. This isn't how the real world works and yet, this is what rewards teach them. It can become a costly form of discipline that teaches values you might not want them to have. So what's the alternative? Consequences.

Are You Calling a Punishment a "Consequence?"

When used incorrectly, "consequences" can make conflict in the home worse! How? Because some Moms are using consequences as a form of punishment. The definition of consequence is simple: the effect that logically or naturally follows from a specific action. Nowhere in my dictionary does consequence have anything to do with punishment. Yet, this is exactly what many Moms are tempted to do. The difference between a consequence and punishment is subtle; yet it is a crucial distinction to make.

The first time I realized that I was using consequences as a form of punishment was on a day *[like many!]* when Grant and Graham were fighting. Grant accused Graham of taking more than his fair share of computer time and Graham fought back with, "Well, I don't care Grant. I know my time limit and I have only had 45 minutes." They exchanged many exasperated sighs, until Grant broke the "sighing stand-off" with, "Well you know Graham, you'd better watch it because the *consequence* of your action will be no playing with me for a week." To which Graham replied, "And the consequence of that action will be no playing with me for two whole weeks." I was awestruck. Where did they learn to use consequences as a form of punishment? *[Gulp!]* Obviously, from me!

Before we continue, I want to make certain that you understand the difference between a consequence and a punishment. How do you know which is which? The simplest way is to check in with your intentions. If there is a part of you that is thinking, "This will show her!" or "He can't treat me that way," or "She should have known better," chances are you are using a consequence as a form of punishment. To be effective, consequences must be delivered firmly yet gently. The two types of consequences are described in the following box.

Two Kinds of "Ultimate Mom" Consequences:

1. **"Divine Intervention Consequences"**—These are commonly known as "natural consequences." They occur when Mother Nature is allowed to step in and take her course without interference from Mom. Some examples include:
   - Your child is cold after deciding not to wear his jacket.
   - Your child is hungry because she forgot her lunch.
   - Your child is tired after staying up late reading.

2. **"Commonsense Consequences"**—These are also known as "logical consequences." These types of consequences require an intervention by you that is fair, kind, and reasonable. The litmus test to ensure that it makes common sense is to ask yourself: "If I applied this consequence to a friend would it seem reasonable to them?" Some examples include:
   - Turning off the TV when the kids are fighting over what to watch.
   - Having your child clean up the mess they made.
   - Taking your child out of the bath if he is splashing water all over the bathroom.

Consequences that Get You What You Want

"Divine Intervention Consequences" are easy, as there is really nothing you need to do other than get out of the way, keep your mouth shut, and allow the process to take its course. The key is to refrain from nagging, "If you keep horsing around like that someone may get hurt. I mean it. Don't come to me crying if you get hurt!"

A child who forgets her lunch and goes hungry is more apt to remember to bring her lunch in the future, than a child who has her Mom hand-deliver it. Although I know it is so tempting, don't succumb! Despite our fears, one missed lunch is not going to create malnutrition in your child [*she will not suddenly become the poster child for a developing nation*]. It is also more likely that a child who gets cold after not wearing a jacket is more likely to wear one the next time. Also the child who is exhausted ng up all night reading will be more likely to choose to go to bed earlier in the future. These lessons are invaluable and require little of you other than to act as a sounding board: "Yes, when we choose to stay up late we can be tired," or "It was cold today!" or "You must have been really hungry. Good for you, for asking your friends to help you out." So now you can scratch off the following from your Mom to-do list:

- ~~Bring my child their lunch when they forget.~~
- ~~Bring my child their homework when they forget.~~
- ~~Bring a coat for my child after they refuse to wear one.~~

Now that you've crossed those off, let's find the secret to using "Commonsense Consequences" well. **Effectively applying "Commonsense Consequences" can be tricky business and are only one tool out of many! Before you attempt to use "Commonsense Consequences" I invite you to use encouragement** (*Chapter Eight*), **a "Mom's Time-Out"** (*Chapter Nine*) **and the problem solving strategies I suggested using during your "family meeting"** (*Chapter Five*). Many times these are all the remedies you will ever need. If after using these "Ultimate Mom" tools, a consequence seems appropriate then deliver it respectfully. Make certain that it is related to the behavior and makes sense.

How to Keep "Commonsense Consequences" Respectful:

1. **Choose a "Commonsense Consequence" that is Related to Your Child's Behavior**—Grounding and taking away privileges are often unrelated to the misbehavior. For instance, if your child is interrupting, forgets to do their chores or has a temper tantrum, what does taking away their TV time have to do with any of these behaviors? If your consequence is not related, a power struggle is the likely outcome. If your child dawdles when called to dinner, a "commonsense consequence" would be to start without them [*without reheating their food later on!*].

2. **Prepare Your Child**—Give your child fair warning, but only once. Respectfully tell them what you have decided to do. E.g. "I often nag at you to come to dinner. I have decided that I do not like nagging and will only call you once from now on. If you are not at the table within two minutes, I will begin eating without you."

3. **Follow Through with the Consequence**—Do what you said you were going to do without reminders, hints or "chances." **"Chances" only teach our children to not listen to us the first, second and sometimes even the third time!** Call them once. If they do not join you start eating dinner with your spouse or on your own. When they show up, warmly welcome them and continue eating your dinner. If they mention that their food is cold, calmly make a comment like, "Yes, it cooled down. It was hot ten minutes ago." Change the subject and continue to enjoy your meal.

4. **Evaluate**—Be open to making small changes after you have experimented with this process for at least one week. The key to success is that you stay kind, firm and are consistent.

Here are two examples of "Commonsense Consequences" that both my parenting class students and myself have successfully used over the years:

- **"Forgot" to Unload the Dishwasher**—This is a simple challenge when you are committed. Simply share that the dishwasher needs to be cleared before making dinner. If your children forget to unload the dishes do something you really enjoy while waiting. When one of your children (hungry and perhaps cranky) asks you, "When is dinner ready?" Reply with, "Once the dishwasher is emptied." In my experience and the dozens of Moms I've had try this very consequence, refraining from reminders, keeping quiet and then happily making the meal after the dishwasher is emptied are the keys to success.

- **Bedtime Dawdling**—Like many Moms, I found that bedtime was an exhaustive process that could take hours! Once I began my graduate courses on effective parenting I quickly decided that enough was enough! The new rule I implemented was: stories didn't start until the boys were completely ready for bed. At 8 o'clock stories would start for whomever was ready. Then at 8:30 p.m. they had ten minutes to do any last things like quickly pee and get a drink of water before I would tuck them in promptly as 8:40 p.m. The timer was ever so useful! If they were not in bed at 8:40 p.m. it was up to them to tuck themselves in. We also had an agreement that they could stay up for as long as they wanted if they were quiet and in bed. Moms have reported that this works well as their children begin to listen to their body's needs and kids love being given this responsibility.

When using "Commonsense Consequences" like the ones above it is probable that you will experience some short-term discomfort [*almost guaranteed really!*]. My Mom clients who have used "Commonsense Consequences" are all amazed when they find how well it works within a relatively short period of time. They have also found that there are enormous pay-offs as their children learn valuable life-long skills. **Even if it takes two weeks of some grief to remedy a major issue wouldn't it be worth it?**

SAFETY WARNING: Mom Use Consistency!

If you are going to use "Commonsense Consequences" you need to ensure that you are consistent. Following through is one of the most difficult aspects of consequences. There may come a time when you think, "Please don't test me as I don't want to have to follow through with what I said I was going to do."

This was exactly what went through my mind when the boys chose to leave their toys scattered all over the living room floor after I had given them a "Commonsense Consequence." I told the boys that if their toys were not picked up by 7 p.m. I would pick them up for them and give them to a local children's charity. Kindly, I shared that toys are not meant for the floor and can be dangerous. Sure enough, dinner came and went and I started to feel that pit in my stomach, "Please pick up your toys so I don't have to do what I said I would do." I thought. They didn't! And I was left doing the unthinkable. Yup! I picked up those toys and put them in a box to give to charity. The boys yelled, "But we were going to pick them up!" They were both mad and yet, I was committed [*as difficult as it was!*] to my word and doing it in the kindest way possible. They asked for their toys back a couple of times and then never mentioned them again. The great thing? They have always picked up after themselves in the common rooms since!

If you say you are going to do something, do it! If you are not certain that you can follow through then simply don't say it in the first place. Why? **When we say we are going to do something and then don't, we are teaching our children that our words are not to be taken seriously— in effect, we are teaching our kids not to listen to us!**

How to Remind Without Words

Get your "feet" to do most (if not all) of the talking. What do I mean by this? Many Moms feel the need to justify, and explain [*"I told you I was going to..."*] when following though with consequences. When implementing consequences words are rarely needed. **Nagging and reminders can actually be an invitation to our children to do the opposite of what we ask! Save yourself the grief and don't go there!** When you follow through, do so without making a big deal out of it and with as little words as possible. **When you say it once, you are letting your actions speak for you and the lesson becomes all the more powerful.**

Reminding seems to be the method of choice for most Moms—a way of communicating not only to their kids, but to their spouses as well! Things like "Pick up your socks," "Did you remember your lunch?" "Do you have homework?" "How many times do I have to tell you?" "Clean clothes are to be hung up!" **The more you remind, the more you** will need to remind. **Your actions will always speaks louder than your words.**

Get What You Want by Giving Your Child What They Want

Now that we've eliminated the need for nagging, it is time to focus on what could possibly be one of the most useful parenting tools: focusing on what your kids want! Life works in segments of time for your child. From waking up, to watching TV, to eating breakfast, to going to school, to eating their lunch, to playing after school, to having dinner, to having a bath, to having stories. Knowing your child's general routine is all you need to help them get what they want while you get what you want.

How? By focusing on the benefits of doing what you want so they can get to what they want. If you are want your child to clean up the game they have been playing; yet, know that they are already thinking about the next segment of time which is listening to their favorite music, you might say something like, "Before you go and enjoy your music you *get* to put the game away." Keep your tone happy and use language that is supportive like "get to" rather than phrases such as "have to."

It's pretty much guaranteed that they will say, "Can't I do it later?" Continue to focus upon the benefit: "The quicker you clean up, the quicker you will be able to enjoy your music. Now what will you put away first?" The more upbeat you can keep your tone, the more upbeat the outcome tends to be.

Spilled Milk: Everyday Teachable Moments

Aside from you, your kids' best teacher is life itself. Sometimes the consequences of our children's actions are so obvious that we feel the need to tell them over and over again what will happen if they do. Yet, if you have ever experienced a friend or spouse using the "I told you so" approach you probably know first-hand just how truly ineffective this approach is in motivating change!

Kids' messes, spills, and even fooling around are all opportunities to learn! Children who are given the opportunity to clean up their own spills learn that they can do something about their accidents. **Taking the time to support children in learning how to clean up a spill or broken glass makes them part of the solution.** Getting them involved is easy when using a simple lesson like, "Mistakes happen. Now you get to clean it up. What do you want to do? Sweep, use the dustpan or both?" Far too many "Super Moms" do for their children what is important for their children to learn. Involving your children is key to their learning and teaches them how to do it on their own. Taking the time to train now means less work for you in the future—this is where your job as Mom can really pay off! Don't rob yourself of this. Don't rob your children of the pride they will feel from learning useful skills.

Chapter Tips:

1. Life is the best teacher. By giving your children the opportunity to learn from "Divine Intervention Consequences" you are respecting them and also assisting them in becoming more responsible.

2. "Commonsense Consequences" always work best when you have clearly told your children in a kind and firm way what you are going to do before you act.

3. Follow through on what you say you are going to do. Going back on your word only teaches your children to not listen to you in the future!

Taking Action:

1. Decide to use one "Divine Intervention Consequence" with your children this week. For example, if they don't want to wear a jacket—don't make them! Here are some "Divine Intervention Consequences" that I am inspired to use:

_____

_____

_____

_____

_____

_____

_____

_____

2. Decide to use one "Commonsense Consequence" within the next week. Go through this chapter and use an example that inspired you. Here are some "Commonsense Consequences" that I am inspired to use:

_____

_____

_____

_____

_____

_____

_____

_____

_____

_____

3. Look for "teachable moments" during this week and support your children in learning from their mistakes.

Dear Diary,

A week ago, Paul asked me what he and his wife should do with their seven year-old-daughter who was having reoccurring nightmares that were preventing her (and therefore her parents) from sleeping. I suggested supporting Kate in focusing on what she wants, rather than on what she doesn't want. My recommendation included asking her to draw a picture of her bad dream and then asking a few questions. Like "What does the 'scary guy' need so he will go away? How can you give him this while staying safe?" Then I suggested she draw a new picture of how she would transform her dream into a beautiful one. Afterwards, I suggested they ask her if she was ready to let go of her bad dream picture, and recycle or throw it into the fireplace. I just received this update:

"Kelly, I want to thank you so very much. I did the drawing exercise with Kate re: her bad dreams and it worked. She drew one of her bad dreams and then another with how it would look as a good dream. Then she chose to burn it in the fireplace and we did it. It was all pretty low key and simple and we did it right before bed. She woke up and said, "no bad dreams." Then later that day I heard her call out her window to our sitter who was just arriving, "Hey Amparo, guess what? I have no more bad dreams. They're all gone!" That was five days ago. So cool. Thank you so much. I've used drawing or list making with my children, but this was perfect. Seriously, thanks a lot. I really appreciate the help (I'm sure you can totally understand). Have a great day! Leslie"

Kelly

How you can MASTER THE TOUGH STUFF FROM TANTRUMS TO SEX

How to Use Quick Comebacks that Work

"Because I said so!" is a comeback that rarely works for long. "Yeah, but that isn't fair!" your child will yell. "Well, well,..." You stutter, searching for an explanation to prove that what you are doing is fair, but the words don't come. Sometimes that "ultimate comeback" just doesn't slip off the tongue like you might want it to. And that's OK! Moms do not need to have the perfect answers because Moms are not perfect. **Moms do the best they can, with what they've got.**

When under stress you may feel pressure to make an instant decision to fulfill your children's requests. Yet an immediate answer is rarely needed. Using avoidance tactics such as, "Go ask your dad." are also unhelpful. Guess what, Mom? You don't have to respond right away! **Instead you can use the following quick comebacks that will give you the time to effectively respond:**

- "That's a good question. I'll need to think about it."
- "Sell me on the idea. I am not yet convinced that it is a good one."
- "I can see that this is really important to you. Write it down on the 'family meeting' agenda and we will discuss it then."
- "I am too tired to give you my 100% attention now. Let's continue this discussion after dinner once I have eaten and can really listen to you in the way that you deserve."

- "What do you think you should do?"

Buy time until you are ready to respond. Ideally, you want to be rested when dealing with your children's concerns; especially when you are dealing with the "tough stuff." This chapter offers guidelines to help you with some of the common "tough stuff" out there.

When making suggestions to Moms I will inevitably hear "Wow, that might work." Then they ask, "How did you come up with that?" Remember, I had the advantage of three years of studying much of this material in graduate school and had parenting experts at my disposal! Then I tried it all and had other Moms do the same. This chapter is dedicated to sharing with you the many practical strategies Moms and I have successfully used.

Rise and Shine, Time to Get Up! DID YOU HEAR ME?

Are you your child's human alarm clock? **Unless there is something medically wrong with your child, I am convinced that *all* children can wake up on their own. The reminders, prodding and screaming that occur in households throughout the nation are a waste of valuable "Mom-ming" energy.** With the boys, it was Graham who got up promptly with his alarm, while Grant snoozed right through. Yet, when there was something exciting (like a trip planned) Grant was the first up!

The best approach I have found for encouraging children to consistently get them up and at 'em is this:
- **Get them an alarm clock or have them use the one they already have.** Consider giving one to them as a gift. Let them know that they are old enough to get themselves up. By the time they enter kindergarten they are usually more than ready.
- **Tell them that it is their responsibility to get themselves up.** Let them know what time you will be in the car ready to leave.
- **Prepare to be late for the first week.** Plan for delays so your mornings are stress-free!

- **Ignore your need to wake them up.** Despite that little voice telling you to get your children up, do your best to enjoy some quiet time reading the paper, examining your belly button, or starting that book *[of the dozens that might be next to your bed!]*.

- **Allow your children to experience the "Divine Intervention Consequences" of sleeping in.** Take the extra time to do something just for you. If they are running around rushing, be supportive, but do not get caught up in the flurry. They may not have time to make their lunch, they might be late for school, or they may miss the bus. That's OK! This is all part of the learning process.

- **Do the same thing the next day and the next day after that.** Be consistent and watch how your children will begin to change their am routine!

It took Grant only three mornings of sleeping in to make the changes that allowed him to be on time at least 98% of the time.

When the Volume of Fighting in the Car is so Loud You Can't Think

This is one of the easiest remedies for Moms to do! I know because I've tried it and countless other Moms in my workshops have too. Read about Meredith's experience in my diary entry *(Chapter Eleven)*. Before I used this technique there was more than one time when one of the boys' arms came flying at me during one of their boxing matches in the car. It was a great relief when I found the following:

- **Tell your kids some variation of: "Just to let you know, I have decided to no longer drive when there is fighting in the car."** Be clear with them, "From now on, if you choose to fight I will immediately pull over until you both show me and tell me that you are ready to go."

- **Prepare for them to test you**. Leave early for the next couple of days when traveling in the car. Bring along a good crossword puzzle, portable project *[knitting anyone?]*, or an enthralling book *[like the one you might be reading right now for instance ☺].*

- **As soon as they start to fight, immediately pull over WITHOUT SAYING A WORD.** Read, write or daydream without paying them any attention.
- **Once they have told you and showed you that they are ready, continue on your journey.** Smile. Be ready to pull over immediately if they choose to start fighting again.

Liar, Liar Pants on Fire: What to do When Your Kid is Lying

It can be extremely upsetting to find out that your child has been lying. Suddenly you imagine the very worst about where this behavior may lead *[Enron, scam artist, or even prison!].* Dr. Oscar Christensen offered the best solution to this behavior that I have heard yet. The response he would use was something like the following, "You are such a wonderful story teller. Would you please write your stories down in this special book so we can share them with others?" This option simply encourages the child's storytelling in a positive way. Again, misbehavior stems from a feeling of discouragement. How could something be more encouraging than asking your child to use their natural talent to create stories for others to enjoy? You never know where this behavior could take them in terms of future careers: screenplay writer, author, or even lawyer *[did I just say that?].*

What to Do When "The Dog Ate Your Kid's Homework"

Homework is one of those "hot topics!" Many Moms feel it is their life purpose to ensure their child completes their homework and correctly. Telling your child that they will get nowhere in life without school is an ineffective lie. Let me save you the grief—don't go there! Don't use this excuse because your child will call you on it as soon as they find out that people like Bill Gates were school dropouts!

Amanda, a past counseling client, was guilted into getting straight A's in school while her parents groomed her for a career in medicine. All she wanted to do was act. When I met her in second-year university she

was on antidepressants, had suicidal thoughts, and had failing gr
The amount of pressure parents place on their children can lead them
to eventually rebel. A-students, when unhappy, can start skipping class,
taking drugs, or even dropping out. **Not every kid on this earth can be
(or should be) a doctor or a lawyer.** We need a variety of skilled adults for
a healthy economy. Those who are the true "success stories" are making
money doing what they love. **One of the best ways Moms can support
their children is by encouraging their children's passions.**

How do you get children to do their homework? You don't! You leave
homework up to your children and let them deal with the consequences
that their teachers provide. When report cards come out, sit down with
them and ask them how they feel about their marks. Which areas do they
want to improve and which areas are they proud of? Ask them about their
interests and ask to see their projects. Attend all school events and parent-
teacher interviews. Aside from showing interest, it is essential to leave the
responsibility of their schoolwork up to them. **In order for children to
do well in the school over the long term, they need to care about their
homework more than you do.** If not, there may come a day when they
forget about it all together—just like my client Amanda.

What to do When Your Child "Forgot to Practice Music"

When your child's violin playing sounds like a dying cat and you
know they haven't practiced, what is your best approach? Use a similar
strategy to the homework scenario above. **If you care about their music
lessons more than your child cares about them you are headed for
struggle.** Were you ever made to take music lessons that you didn't enjoy?
Are you doing same thing to your child?

Grant and Graham were both taking piano lessons but would
"forget" to practice more and more frequently. The thing that made the
most difference was this:

- **Let your child know that music lessons require that he
  practice "X" number of minutes per day.** Kindly share that
  you have noticed that he has not been regularly practicing

and want to know if he would like to continue taking music lessons.

- **Discuss it with him.** He may tell you that music lessons are important but be prepared for him to tell you that it is not. If this is the case find something else he is excited about or simply give him the extra time to play.
- **Implement a "Commonsense Consequence."** If he chooses to continue taking music lessons let him know that if he decides not to practice or forgets to practice (for whatever reason) during the week, you will cancel his lesson.
- **Follow through.** If he "forgets" do not use reminders. Cancel the lesson on his behalf. When he asks you why you aren't ready to take him to practice calmly ask: "What was our agreement about your music lessons?" If he gets upset *[and he probably will!]*, validate his feelings, "You are feeling mad that I cancelled your music lesson."
- **Continue this process next week.** Follow through. Remain kind and firm.

Curfew? What Curfew?

Curfew is a big trigger because Moms want to ensure their kids safety. It is essential to have clear boundaries and give your children the opportunity to discuss alternatives when it comes to curfews. Here is what I suggest:

- **Set a time.** Be certain that it is clear.
- **Discuss what you want them to do if they are late.** Have them call you by telephone so you don't worry. If they need a ride home or are in danger, ask them to call you *[if this happens make certain that you don't yell at them the entire ride home!]*.
- **Discuss the "Commonsense Consequences" of being late.** A common one is setting their curfew one hour earlier until they show you that they can be responsible with following the set time. Once they do this, go back to their original curfew time. It is important that this is not used as a punishment. You may

also decide to give them the option of having their friends over in your home until their regular curfew.

What to Do When You've got Five Minutes to Get Across Town and Your Kid is Still in Their Pajamas

This suggestion freaks more than a few Moms out. Use this strategy only after feeling confident in your abilities to follow though with what you said you were going to do. For some Moms having their child spend the day in their P.J.'s at school can feel like a total embarrassment. If this is the case, then skip this section all together.

When it comes to being ready, your child has a choice. As soon as you know that you are pressed for time, let your child know how much time there is before you will leave. For a young child, give her a five-minute warning. Let her know that you will leave on time and take her in her pajamas if she has not dressed. For an older child (*old enough to be left home alone*) let them know that you would love to take her to school but if she is not in the car in five minutes you will go without her. Follow through with a smile on your face—this is key for this method to be effective. You are not being unreasonable or punitive you simply choose not to be late—period.

You might choose to come back for your older child later if you have the time. For your younger child, happily drop them off at school in their pajamas. Worried about embarrassment? No need to be. This was your child's choice and is a natural consequence of *her* decision—the best kind of learning there is! You might be amazed to find that your kid actually becomes a celebrity for a day as they show off their P.J.'s to the entire school.

How to Handle Your Young Child Who Runs Away from You in the Street

When it comes to physical safety, you are the adult. If there is a dangerous situation there is no question that you need to do whatever is necessary to keep your child safe. Keeping a child safe does not include yelling at them for being stupid! When it comes to safety, prevention is the best method. This comes through training and teaching. Spend time doing just this. Ask your child to bring one of the cans from the recycling bin and have him place the containers under the wheels of your car. Then take your child away from the car while you get someone to drive over them. Once the car has stopped, go up and examine the containers. Ask him what he thinks would happen to him if he were under the car. Then practice crossing the street starting with quiet streets and then moving to busier ones encouraging them with comments like, "Great job at looking both ways!"

Resolving Bedtime Struggles Once and for All

Bedtime is an epidemic problem that plagues most households each and every night. If it's not one more story, it's "ten more minutes" of their favorite show, or it's dawdling in the bathroom. Grant and Graham were pros at stalling. One evening when I was out they managed to get a friend of mine to let them stay up for two and a half hours past their bedtime! Once this friend found out my approach he was never conned again. So here it is:

- **Tell Her What You are Going to Do.** Say something like, "Sometimes I feel frustrated when bedtime takes longer than it needs to be. From now on I will be at your bedside promptly at ____pm to tuck you in. If you are not ready to be tucked in I will get ready for bed myself. If you would like a hug you can come and find me for a quick one, but I will not return to your room."

- **Follow Through.** As discussed be in her room on time. Give her one five-minute warning although it is not necessary. If your child is not ready, leave. Be prepared to keep your mouth shut regardless of tears, angry words, or pleads to be tucked in. Give one hug [if they ask] then continue with your tasks. If your child tries to get you involved simply say, "I'll be happy to speak with you in the morning. Sweet dreams." That is all.

What to Do When there's a Boogieman
Under Your Kid's Bed

Fears are natural and your children will face many throughout their lifetime. The best thing you can do is to help them learn to deal with the fear! Take the time to understand the fear and validate their feelings. Stay firm on the need for them to stay in their own room. Find ways of making it safe. Each time your children come into your room, take them back to their own room. Stay with them for a couple of minutes. Tell them that you have faith in their ability to handle the situation. Instead of telling them that there is no boogieman, ask them what the boogieman is like, why he is there, and what he wants. Brainstorm with your children possible ways to live together peacefully with the Boogieman. You can suggest writing the boogieman a note, or visualizing a magical fortress that protects your children's beds. When they make it through a night on their own encourage each of them: "I noticed that you made it through an entire night on your own. You must have been proud of yourself. How did you do that?"

What to Do When Your Child Says:
"You Don't Love Me as Much as You Love _____."

When your child accuses you of not loving them as much as you love their sibling, what can you do? The boys Mom experienced this exact situation when Grant began saying things like, "You don't love me as much as you love Graham." When a child questions their Mother's love, Moms often feel the need to justify and defend themselves. This approach only exasperates the problem since the more you defend, the more you are giving him evidence that he might be right.

It was my teacher and mentor, Dr. Oscar Christensen, who made a suggestion that works like a charm. He recommended making light of the issue by laughing and saying, "You are so funny," and then giving him a pat on the arm and go on with whatever you are doing. This is far better than defending yourself, "Of course I love you! I love you the same as your sister. Do you think I went through 18 hours of labor for nothing!" If you take the comment seriously this only gives him reason to suspect it is a problem. Now, if it continues to persist over a long period of time you may want to ask things like, "Is what you are really wanting a hug from me?" Don't fall into the trap of discussing it in a way that justifies it. Ask him, "What do you need right now to feel more connected to me?" Sometimes a hug is all that is needed.

For those of you who still question if this will work, allow me to finish the story about Grant. One morning Grant said to me, "My Mom doesn't love me as much as she loves Graham." I replied, "You are so funny Grant! You know she loves you." He broke out into a smile that said, "Of course I do." Then he quickly recovered and said, "No, she doesn't." I then said, "You've got a great sense of humor Grant!" He laughed and I never heard him say it again. Bringing out the humor put his concerns to rest. My very reaction told him that I didn't believe his fears for an instant.

Let's Talk About the Birds and Bees

This is probably one of the most important ongoing discussions you will have with your children. When they start asking questions it is critical that you answer them *[even when you are turning two shades of red!]*. Here are the basic guidelines:

- **Call a Sex Organ a Sex Organ.** Instead of only using slang words such as "private part," "willie," "weenie," "big kahuna," "foofoo," and "sacred spot," get used to referring to a penis as a "penis" and a vagina as a "vagina." Using words other than the proper names can suggest that there is something dirty or wrong. If you are uncomfortable they can easily pick up on this. All it takes is practice!

- **Answer Their Questions Honestly.** When they ask you where babies come from, discuss it to the capacity they can understand. Go to the library and take out books on the subject. When you see sex or nudity in TV or in films discuss it *[gulp!]* as openly as possible.

- **Be Open.** When we are open they will ask. If we are not they won't ask. Instead they will learn about sex from their friends,

TV, and the Internet! Therefore it is up to us. Talk about your views on sex before marriage, talk about pregnancy and birth control, and discuss AIDS and STD's. Even take a few field trips to volunteer centers that deal with these issues. Encourage them to keep asking questions.

It is a myth that the more our children know the more they will do. It is when they are not informed that they tend to do things they later regret because they simply weren't aware of the consequences. It is part of your job to inform them. Which would you rather? Do you want to deal with a pregnant daughter, a son who is a father-to-be or a little embarrassment discussing things like condoms and oral sex now?

Till Death Do Us Part: How to Handle Grief

Part of life is death. For parents this can be an extremely difficult subject, especially when it comes to handling our kids. At some point in our children's life they will need to deal with the loss of a loved one. As Mothers, we may just want to kiss that "owie" and make it go away. Yet, in order to fully heal we need to honor the "owie" and the process of grieving that comes along with it.

There are seven main aspects to cover when a death, which is very similar to divorce, occurs. These are:

- **Ensure that You get the Support You Need.** Too often a child can inappropriately become the caregiver. Getting the support you need enables you to be there for your child. This is the very reason that airlines request that you put on your oxygen mask before helping your child to put on theirs. We cannot be effective when we haven't taken care of ourselves. Make certain you are getting the help you need.
- **Ask Your Child if They Would Like to Attend the Funeral or Memorial.** We forget that often our child does know what is best. If she decides to attend, make it clear that she can leave at any time. Have someone that you, and your child, trusts to be there for her and take her away if she decides

she wants to leave. Have an alternative plan ready e.g. going to the park, watching a favorite video, reading a good book, drawing etc.

- **Explain Death in Terms of Your Spiritual Beliefs.** Share your beliefs about what happens in death as you understand it. Be prepared for questions and enlist the help of a priest, minister, rabbi, etc. Ensure that the explanations are not scary, fearful, or anxiety producing.

- **Assure Your Child of Your Love and Support.** It is normal for a child to wonder what will happen to her when you die. Have a plan and share it. Remind your child that love does not die. Use the example of when you are not with her (i.e. when you are at work and she is at school) that you still love one another.

- **When Communicating Listen More than You Talk.** Give her the opportunity to share her feelings, assuring her that it is perfectly OK to cry and feel sad. When we lose someone—it hurts. Plan for this talk to take place over time. Questions may surface for your child the more that time goes by. Be open to receiving them and remember to listen from your heart, rather than from your head.

- **Play with the Grief.** Use clay, puppets, dolls, or stuffed animals to act out the story of loss with your child. Ask questions like, "Who is going to play you?" "Who is going to play me?" "What is the saddest part of the story?" This can go a long way in helping her to express her grief and share it with you. Also, get out and have some fun together—throw a ball around, go for a walk and play.

- **Create a Ritual Together.** Some of the wonderful ways of dealing with grief includes writing a letter or drawing a picture for the one who has just recently passed on. Consider including pictures. Share your favorite memories while creating it together. It can even be helpful to sit down together and write a letter back from the one who has passed away. Ask your child what her relative or pet would want to say to him.

Grieving is part of the "tough stuff" and is an important process of life. The range of emotions is natural. With time the sorrow can be transformed into happy memories that remind us that we loved and were loved—one of the most important things in life.

Chapter Tips:

1. Kids rarely need an immediate answer to any of their questions. When you don't know how to respond take the time you need to think about it.
2. If you want something for your children more than they do, you may be headed for conflict in the future.
3. When it comes to the "tough stuff" clear and open communication, follow through, and consistency are the keys to success.

Taking Action:

1. Choose one of the specific solutions from this chapter that you are excited about and apply it!
2. Does talking about sex embarrass you? Talk about it with a friend, partner or counselor and see if you can't find a way to ease the discomfort.
3. Is there someone in your life who has passed on that you would like closure with? If so write them a letter, paint them a picture, or do some sort of good-bye visualization where you tell them everything you need to. Consider having them write you back by writing it yourself!

Dear Diary,

Just came back from a session with a client "Charlotte" who is finding the transition to parenthood stressful on her marriage. It reminded me of what one friend's mother in-law said: "It's only twenty years, dear, and then you get your life back." How uninspiring! Will a marriage be intact in twenty years? Judging from current data as many as 50% won't, and I wonder how many of the remaining 50% are truly happy?

Charlotte shared that she has become short tempered when it comes to her husband. She doesn't understand why "Matthew" can't "see" the dirt that she does. And sex? Once a year would more than satisfy her needs. Yet, "Matthew" isn't happy about being last on a long list of "to do" items. It wasn't that long ago that they couldn't keep their hands off one another. Now he has entered what he calls the "long cold winter"—no fire, no passion and no sex. He loves his son, but wants his wife, his lover, and his best friend back. Even though Charlotte trusts Matthew completely, she says she now understands why some husbands are suddenly "tempted'" by that cute secretary. By the end of our session she came to the conclusion that "date nights" are definitely in order. As much as she loves her son and wants to spend time with him, she also wants him to grow up in a family that is held together by a happy marriage.

How different would families be if husbands treasured their wives, and wives equally treasured their husbands? How much more would parents give to their children in terms of love, support, and joy when they themselves were experiencing a nurturing and intimate partnership? This is the missing piece many families are seeking.

Kelly

DARING TO DEAL WITH DADS

Dad as Part of Your Childrens' Lives

Dads can be a wonderful thing in our childrens' lives. Though sometimes, as is the case with Grant and Graham *[their dad abandoned them at a young age]*, it can be one of the most challenging. Wherever you are on this spectrum, it is essential that Moms do their best to support the dads in their kids' lives. **Dads, like Moms, thrive when truly appreciated. Just as it is with our children, it is important that we start honoring dads for who they are.** We can do this by showing our appreciation for all that they do, by specifically asking for what we want *[they need and often want this!]*, and by being gentle with them when they make mistakes.

It is also important that we support healthy relationships between our kids and their dad. Each relationship will be different. The following pages present a list of general guidelines that can help you support your children's dad—no matter what his role may be. Doing so will only further support your children.

For a Loving and Involved Dad Who Lives with You:

- **Encourage**—Focus on what dad is doing well rather than on what you believe he is doing wrong.
- **Ask for What You Want**—Dads are not mind readers! Instead of "nagging" or dropping hints *[that they may never pick up on!]*

make specific requests. Spell it out word for word in a pleasant and loving way.

- **Give Your Kids Special Time with Their Dad**—Support your children and their dad in doing things together. Take this time to do nurturing things that support you.
- **Accept Your Parenting Differences**—"You say potato, I say potŏto. You say tomato; I say tomŏto..." This song exemplifies the different parenting approaches you and dad may have. Rest assured your kids will adapt to each style and will know what they can get away with and with whom. Ask your spouse to consider learning this new parenting style with you. Be prepared for them to say "no." It is essential that you do not pressure them. Keep the door open for them to change their mind.
- **Spend Weekly Fun Time as a Family**—Have regular fun "family dates." A great time is after your "family meetings."
- **Look for Ways to Appreciate Dad**—Greet him at the door with a big "I missed you" hug *[even on the days that you may not feel like it]*. Tell him how loved he is on a daily basis. You can't show your appreciation enough!
- **Go on Weekly Dates**—In order to maintain a joyful partnership and marriage, ensure that you are taking the time (at least once a week) to just *be* together as a couple. No time? Make the time! This one act alone can strengthen your relationship and give your children a model of a healthy partnership. **We need more healthy couples in this world! Choose to become one.** Remember that once your children have left home, you will be left or "stuck" with one another *[for some of you this may be a scary thought!]*. Make certain that your significant other is one of your best friends now *instead of just a roommate!*

Dad Lives with You but has Limited Time for the Kids:

- **Discuss Your Concerns in a Supportive Way**—Ask dad if he is happy with the relationship he has with you and his children. Listen to him. Look for ways to have quality family time together no matter what is going on. Let him know how much quality time together means to you. If dad travels a lot purchase a calling card and have him call you and the kids every night.

- **Have "Family Meetings"**—Use "family meetings" to come together once a week as a family. Discuss at your meeting how to create more time with dad. Always end the meeting with a fun event that everyone can enjoy.
- **Review and Create Your Life Goals Together**—If you don't know where you are going or what your priorities are in life *[for instance, quality time with your kids and quality time together!]* you will never get there. Identify what is truly important to both of you. Clarify the changes needed to get you on track and keep you there.

Dad Does Not Live with You but You have a Civil Relationship:

- **Be Clear**—When it comes to visitation be clear. Always ask yourself, "What is best for the kids?"
- **Check in with Your Kids**—Regularly discuss with your children how they are feeling about visits. Be clear that both dad and you only want what is best for them. Listen to their opinion even if it includes seeing you less. Do your best to accommodate and try out their suggestions.
- **When Your Kids Come Home after Being with Dad, be Excited!**—When your kids tell you about all the great things they did while with dad you may feel jealous or resentful. Perhaps, he can afford more than you or it seems that he gets all the fun, while you get all the discipline. This dynamic only makes kids feel guilty. Enjoy their happiness. Focus on the fun things that you can do with your kids. It's never about the money or the activity; it's about the quality time you spend with them.

- **If You have a Question for Dad Ask Him, don't go Through the Kids**—Call dad or write down your questions rather than making your children "messengers."

Dad Does Not Live with You and it is a Difficult Relationship:

- **Work on Forgiving Him**—Even though you may want to throw-up every time you hear his name, it is essential that you work on forgiving him *[this does not mean condoning what he did or what he does by the way!]*. Let go for your own sake. Resentment, anger, and sorrow only breed emotional upset for you and your child—it is time to move on!

- **Consider a Child Therapist**—When it comes to difficult father-child relationships, a child therapist can provide a safe place for your child to share freely. Keep in mind that your child needs to like the therapist in order for it to work!

- **Support Your Child in Having a Good Relationship with Dad**—If dad is safe for your child to be around, do everything in your power to support a healthy relationship between the two of them. Your issues may have nothing to do with the relationship he has with your child.

- **Discuss Facts, Not Judgments**—Stay away from passing judgments and calling dad names. Even if it is true, it will only hurt your child.

- **Listen to Your Child Instead of Using "I Told You So"**—If your child ever comes home upset after a visit with their dad just listen. Refrain from jumping on the bandwagon with "I told you so." Keep these comments to yourself and focus on your child's feelings. Encourage them to share the issue and solve it with their dad.

- **Keep Your Child Safe**—If there is any known violence, alcoholism, or sex abuse your first goal is to do everything in your legal power to keep your child safe. Seek legal consultation if need be.

A Missing Dad:

- **Get Counseling Support**—This is often the key that can help mend broken hearts—yours and your child's.

- **Speak Kindly of Dad**—Your anger and resentment, no matter how justified; will do more damage to you and your child than it will ever do to dad. Everyone on this earth has gifts [granted sometimes incredibly hidden]. Your job is to find your ex's strengths and share these with your child. It doesn't need to be syrupy sweet—only the truth. Remember what you once loved about their dad so you can experience healing.

- **Validate Your Kids Feelings**—A missing dad is hurtful. Acknowledge this hurt and support your child in seeing that even a parent can make mistakes—sometimes BIG mistakes.

- **Forgive**—Use the suggestions in the forgiveness section further on in this chapter and choose to forgive dad. Help your child to do the same.

Getting Clear on What You Want and Who You Want to be in Your Romantic Relationship

The person we want our romantic partner to become is the person we need to become. It is easy to point fingers at what they are doing wrong. Yet, we may not realize that when we point our index finger at dad we've usually got our last three fingers pointing back at us! When we play the game of, "Once he finally does what I want him to do—then I will do what he wants" no one wins. **The more we focus on the qualities we like in dad, the more we will experience these positive qualities. It needs to start with us.**

No matter if you are married, single, or in between; getting clear on what you want, and who you want to be, will help you to create your ideal relationship. After the break up of a "roller coaster" relationship that lasted six years, I wrote out a list of 45 qualities that I wanted in my next relationship. I began demonstrating them in myself. Five months later, the man of my dreams showed up exhibiting every item on that list! You know what? Be that which you seek and then be open to it showing up!

Why You May Choose to Forgive the Unforgivable

What often prevents us from creating a fulfilling relationship is the resentment we hang onto. Forgiveness—such a simple word, yet it can take an entire lifetime to achieve. Forgiveness is sometimes believed to be a weakness, rather than a strength that leads to peace of mind. When we choose to forgive we are doing our health, our future, and our kids a big favor. **Forgiveness is not about ignoring your pain or even excusing the act. It is about taking a bold step forward. It is choosing to no longer burden yourself with pain in response to what someone else did (or what you perceived them to do). It is about courageously choosing a path to your own healing, so you can finally get on with the life you deserve to live!**

Forgiveness of self and others is impossible when we insist upon fairness in every aspect of our lives. When the score is uneven, when it is not fair, that is often when we need to forgive the most. Our society justifies revenge, but this only keeps us in our misery. To forgive and forget is not always necessary. Sometimes it is even immoral, but healing our heart through forgiveness and grace is always necessary. Human beings are not perfect—none of us are. We all make mistakes. Choose to remember this.

Four Simple Ways to Forgive: for Your Sake and Your Kids

Forgiveness can revitalize our life, and create a clean slate in which we can love again. When we hold onto hurt we do not have space for love to come into our life. When this happens our whole family suffers needlessly. So how do we let go?

Here are Four Simple Ways to Forgive:

1. **Ask for forgiveness and forgive your loved ones on a daily basis.** Let go of any residual anger through writing, sharing (respectfully, of course), and looking for solutions.

2. **Seek clarity during times of conflict.** Ask yourself, "Is it more important to get back at this person or is it more important to be happy?"

3. **Take responsibility for your own part in the problem.** Sometimes the person we are most mad at is our self. Perhaps we are angry at what we have allowed to happen or for not listening to our intuition. Forgive yourself. Learn from your mistakes.

4. **Send blessings to those that have done you wrong.** When you direct negative thoughts toward another silently say to yourself: "Peace be with you, as it is with me. I wish you blessings of health, happiness, and abundance."

Are You Really Ready to Forgive?

Before you are able to forgive (and use the forgiveness visualization that is included in the next section) you have to want to forgive. Here are four questions that will help you to determine whether or not you truly want to forgive:

- Do I choose to accept the fact that I, like everyone else, am an ordinary human being who makes mistakes?
- Have I suffered enough from this incident?
- Is it possible that this situation could make me stronger?
- Am I ready to forgive this person knowing that they too are human?

If you have answered the above questions with "yes," you are ready to move on to the next section that describes how to do the forgiveness visualization. If you have not answered "yes" to each of the four questions above, here some others to ask yourself:

- What will it take for me to let go and start living my life?
- How does holding onto the pain serve me?

- What is preventing me from letting this go?
- How could I benefit from letting this go?
- Would my children benefit if I were to let this go?

Think about your answers. Consider writing a letter to the person you need to forgive—expressing your anger, disappointment, and frustration. Burn or recycle it later. Rarely is it in your best interest to actually send it to the person. You may choose to work through your pain with a trained therapist. Whatever you decide, I encourage you to make a commitment to start the process today.

How to Use the "Forgiveness Visualization"

Know that you have the power to use the "forgiveness visualization" to release regret, guilt, hurt, and all the other emotions and beliefs that may be holding you back. Read the following "forgiveness visualization" or create your own audio version by recording it.

The "Forgiveness Visualization:"

Find a place where you can sit or lie down quietly without being disturbed. Close your eyes and take a long deep breath from down deep in your belly. Choose a color that represents forgiveness and another that represents pain. Each time you inhale, see yourself inhaling the color of forgiveness. Send this breath through your entire body. As you exhale visualize yourself exhaling the color you have chosen to represent your pain. As you inhale, inhale feelings of love, healing, peace, fulfillment, and joy. As you exhale, exhale disappointment, frustration, anger, resentment—any emotion or belief that may hold you back from letting this issue go. Continue to focus on your breathing, inhaling forgiveness, and exhaling pain. Continue until you have let go of all of your pain.

Now, bring the person you want to forgive to mind and continue to breathe. Fill yourself with love and allow this love to expand until it reaches the other person as well. Say to them, "I choose to forgive you now and forever." Say this three times. Don't be surprised if part of your mind says, "No way!" Thank that voice for sharing, and stay with the visualization. Now say, "I choose to completely forgive you for anything that happened in our relationship, intentional and unintentional that caused me pain. Every negative thought, word and deed I forgive you. I fully forgive myself. I am free and you are free. It is a joyous feeling." Past scenes may come to you. Let the love you are experiencing flow to those scenes. Notice what you learned from each situation. Express your gratitude for this learning by saying: "Thank you for opening my heart and mind to accept love, forgiveness, and understanding." If at any time you experience hurt focus again on your breath inhaling forgiveness and exhaling any grief.

Now say to yourself, "I deserve to let this go. Deep within my heart I choose to forgive you as I forgive me. I deserve to let this hurt go and to forgive myself for any hurt I have caused anyone else. I do this freely, joyously, and lovingly. I release you completely; I release the pain of your actions. We are now free— you and I. This is wonderful." Bless this person as you watch them fade away. Stay with your breath, until you are ready to return to the room with eyes open.

Easy Ways of Finding Healthy Male Role Models

Forgiveness is key to finding awesome male role models. If you have any resentment that has built up toward men it may be preventing you from attracting the great ones. The success of our daughters and our sons rests in part upon having positive role models—both female and male. Our kids can't ever have too many role models!

It is your beliefs about men that will directly determine what kind of men you attract in to your life. Take a good look at which men you have let in. If your life is filled with caring men—perhaps the new "metro sexual" man who is defined as a guy who has both sensitivity and masculinity [*he even likes shopping, I hear!*]; then chances are you have positive beliefs about men. However, if you don't yet have these men in your life, or you would like more, consider the following.

Five Ways to Attract Role Models:

1. Sign your child up for a program like Big Brothers where sons are paired with (pre-screened) role models.

2. Alter your perceptions of men by using a daily affirmation like, "I easily attract supportive and caring men."

3. Read and share positive stories about men with your kids. Encourage them to have positive sport role models; players who are good guys on and off the field.

4. Consider getting your children involved in a team sport with an awesome male coach—there are so many out there.

5. If you are fortunate to have some healthy male family members invite them over regularly!

What to Do when Your Kids Hate Your Date

If you are single and are dating, your kids might not be that supportive at first. One day a boyfriend of mine was visiting us. As we sat in the living room Graham seemed quite cheery but Grant moved to the opposite side of the room with his arms folded over his chest. He had a scowl on his face that made him look like he was ready to do battle. Grant's answers to my boyfriend's questions were abrupt and he was acting rude. He had a good reason—they almost always do.

After a heart-to-heart talk I found out that Grant was mad about a card game that the three of them had played weeks ago. My boyfriend had decided to "cheat" in the game and helped Graham out "illegally." Grant interpreted my boyfriend's actions to mean that he liked Graham more than him. After some prompting, the two of them talked it out. Grant told him why he was angry. My boyfriend sincerely apologized. After thinking about it for a couple of minutes Grant said, "OK, we can be friends again."

When your kids hate your date there is always a reason—so find it! Having had divorced parents myself, I know the feeling of meeting a new date. It is not fun, so be gentle! Until you are in a serious relationship do not invite your date to become a part of the family. This saves your kids from an unnecessary emotional roller coaster ride. It also decreases the chances of your children feeling abandoned if the relationship doesn't work out. Open communication is essential when you are dating. Check in with your children on a regular basis. Be willing to listen, although do not accept disrespect. Discuss what it is that they don't like and what it is that they do. Ensure that you spend quality one-on-one time with your kids even if you are in a serious relationship. If you are in the process of creating a blended family (or introducing a new step-dad) keep the faith that the situation will work out!

For Better and For Worse: Getting Through Tough Times

Whether it is dating, a loss of a job, death in the family, divorce, or just feeling plain depressed, there will inevitably be rough and tough times within your family. During these times make the following list a family STAPLE.

A Family Staple:

1. **S**—Share what's in your heart with girlfriends and dad.

2. **T**—"Time-outs" for Moms can be used to recharge, de-stress, and gain perspective.

3. **A**—Ask for and accept help. Be specific with your needs.

4. **P**—Pray for guidance, clarity, and courage.

5. **L**—Look for the good in dad and tell him what you love.

6. **E**—Encourage yourself, your kids and especially dad.

Chapter Tips:

1. Dad, like your children, flourishes when encouraged. Give him some and watch him shine!

2. Forgiveness does not mean agreeing with another's mistakes. Forgiveness means giving oneself the chance to move on to more wonderful experiences.

3. Surrounding your family with wonderful male role models can be essential to your children's future relationship success.

Taking Action:

1. Do a "male" archeological dig to find out what your beliefs are. Write down five significant men that have been a part of your life. Write down their qualities. Ask yourself, "What must I believe for these men to be in my life?"

   i. _____

   _____

   ii. _____

   _____

   iii. _____

   _____

   iv. _____

   _____

   v. _____

   _____

2. Honor a man in your life today by sending him a card, leaving him a message, or telling him how much he means to you.

3. Say a daily affirmation such as, "Wonderful men are naturally attracted to me." "I deserve to have awesome men in my life." "I choose to have healthy relationships with men." Write down some of the affirmations that you will use below:

_____

_____

_____

_____

_____

_____

_____

_____

_____

_____

_____

Dear Diary,

Just heard a story about a television personality in town who paid his son for household chores. When his son was sixteen and wanted to earn more spending money, this father recommended him to a friend who owned a local full service gas station. On the first week of the job, the manager found this teen doing his homework while a car was waiting to be served. The manager said, "Hey, there's a customer." To which the boy replied, "I'll get to it in a sec." The manager raised his voice, "THERE IS A CUSTOMER!" Promptly the boy replied, "Hey, minimum wage, minimum effort buddy."

Is there a connection between this attitude and being paid for chores at home? Yes! When kids are paid for their chores they begin to expect material compensation for everything they do. When they don't see an immediate material benefit, they can become lazy, aloof, and apathetic. And they ultimately will miss out on the intrinsic satisfaction that comes from a job well done.

Kelly

YOUR KID'S ALLOWANCE— IT'S JUST COMMON CENTS

You are the Person to Teach Your Child About Money!

Is the word "cha-ching" like music to your ears? Do dollar signs make your heart skip a beat? Do they make you queasy? When it comes to money, Moms have a variety of experiences. Like parenting, you may feel like you are sometimes in the "deep end."

Wherever you are at financially, I know one thing about you. I know that you are, without a doubt, the best person to teach your child about money. Why? Like it or not, you are the biggest influence in how your child will handle money in the future. Since it is almost certain that he is not learning about money in school—the responsibility is on you. **If finances are not your cup of tea, fear not, because the best way to learn is to teach.**

When Grant and Graham were nine and eleven years old we started reading them one of my favorite money books called, "Rich Dad, Poor Dad" by Robert Kiyosaki. They listened intently and were eager to soak it up. Soon after, Grant returned home from school one day, and shared that he had an interesting talk with his teacher. He told me this story: "Mr. B told the class today that it's important to get a good job that pays well when you grow up. But I knew that was wrong." "What did you do?" I asked. "I told him that I had been learning that it isn't about getting a job that pays well, but about learning how to manage and invest your money so you can get a job that you love." I couldn't have said it better if I had been there myself. "And what did Mr. B. say?" I asked. "Not much. He was very quiet. So I just left."

Kids grasp practical concepts about money much more quickly than we do. Why? They don't have the accumulated negative beliefs about money holding them back. Learning about money together can establish an awesome bonding opportunity for the two of you. You'll be amazed at their thoughts on the subject and you may just learn a lot from them. This chapter will give you the guidelines that will help you and your children become strong financial managers.

How We Unconsciously Teach Our Kids to Become "Spendaholics"

Many kids today are receiving the wrong impression about managing money. How? **Kids learn the most by what Moms do, rather than what they say. By their actions alone, many Moms are teaching their children to become future "spendaholics" because of what I call the "ATM Phenomenon."** Kids quickly lose the value of a dollar when they witness Mom pulling out the plastic time and again to pay for things. Most young children equate swiping the "plastic"—credit cards and ATM cards—with "free money." Dozens of Moms have shared a variation of the following story with me: child says, "I want that." Mom replies, "I don't have any money." Child trying to be helpful replies, "That's OK just use your card."

It would appear that the belief in "quick and easy money" is becoming rampant. Credit cards can be like drugs in your children's future. And the more they don't learn, the more likely they are to have a spending problem down the road. Fortunately, by spending time now to educate your kids about "plastic," the better off they will be.

How to Involve Your Children in Your Financial Life

"Mind your own business" is a phrase that may come to mind when it comes to the subject of money—especially when dealing with your kids.

Some Moms fear that their children will let their financial secrets "out of the bag" or that information about how much the family earns will give their kids a license to demand more. Why involve your kids in your financial life? Your children are already involved! The less you talk about it, the more you leave it up to their imaginations—dangerous indeed.

Choosing to involve your children in your finances will do two things: 1) it will increase their financial understanding and 2) it will help them become more responsible with their own money. How do you involve them? Be honest and make it as interesting as possible. Remember to stay away from mandatory lectures and stop if you see their eyes glazing over! **Making the decision to introduce your children to your personal finances can happen over time. Build up a certain amount of trust before sharing exactly how much you make and spend.** Watch for the cues that let you know that your children are mature and responsible enough to handle the information. Always look for those "teachable moments," in which you take the time to answer your children's questions about money.

Six Ways to Involve Your Children Financially:

1. **Ask Them for Their Opinion**—For instance, "I've got two thousand dollars to spend on our vacation this year how would you suggest we spend it?" "I'm trying to decide which shampoo to purchase, which would you choose and why?"

2. **Explain How "Plastic" Works in the Money World**—When you are using "plastic" explain what happens, where the money comes from, and how the store gets paid. Make the explanation interesting. Ask things like, "Do you want to discover what happens when Mom uses this card? It may look like magic, but this is what really happens..."

3. **Discuss Your Financial Choices at "Family Meetings"**—At some point show your kids your monthly expenses including any debt and related interest charges. Be patient with their

questions. Show them how you pay your bills and let them help you.

4. **Discuss Their Educational Plans and Your Life Insurance**— Show them the documents and plans. If you haven't bought insurance yet, make it a priority. Let your children deposit the money into their educational savings plan, and take them to your insurance office when you renew.

5. **Discuss Your Will with Them**—This is not a morbid act, but a form of insurance that ensures your kids are taken care of in the unlikely case that you die early. Knowing what a Will entails and who will be given custody can put some of your kid's fears to rest *[no pun intended!]*.

6. **Get Your Own Financial House in Order**—If there are areas of your finances that you want to improve, start the process. Want a little support or guidance? **If you do not yet have my special report called, "Discover the Treasure That Lies in Your Family Pay Check" go to www.ultimateparenting.com /downloads and receive it free.**

Dissolve Your Child's "Money Temper Tantrums"

Allowances can help dissolve "money temper tantrums." "Mom can I have that?" may often turn into "MOM, I WANT THAT!" If you choose to implement an allowance program as described in this chapter you will have an easy and effective answer to "Mom can I have that?" You will smile and in a calm voice ask, "Did you bring your money?" **Kids love being in charge of their own money. Allowances give them the practical experience required to become skillful at managing their own money.**

Why is an allowance given? An allowance is given as a way to promote healthy money management. It is not given as a reward for chores. Chores are an everyday part of being a member of the family and should not be remunerated over and above the thanks they receive for their contribution. **Some Moms wonder, "Why give kids money for free?"** Good questions. **The fact is you already give your children money for free.** How often a week do you dole out money for treats, dinners, entertainment, clothes, toys, books, videos etc.? **Giving an allowance will help you to keep your spending on the kids in check *[can actually save you money!]* while teaching them valuable life skills at the same time.**

Allowance Guideline: an Effective Way to Teach Your Child

When To Start? As soon as your child understands that money is used to buy things she wants, she is ready. This usually happens around the age of three or four. The rule of thumb for deciding how much a weekly allowance will be is usually about $1.00—$2.00 for every year of your child's life. Therefore the approximate allowance would be somewhere in the following range:

Child's Age	Weekly Allowance	Monthly
3	$3.00-$6.00	$12.00-$24.00
4	$4.00-$8.00	$16.00-$32.00
5	$5.00-$10.00	$20.00-$40.00
6	$6.00-$12.00	$24.00-$48.00
7	$7.00-$14.00	$28.00-$56.00
8	$8.00-$16.00	$32.00-$64.00
9	$9.00-$18.00	$36.00-$72.00
10	$10.00-$20.00	$40.00-$80.00
11	$11.00-$22.00	$44.00-$88.00

It is important that you choose an amount that is affordable for you. When you have two or more children be certain to stick with a formula like the one shown above; thus keeping it fair.

When are Allowances Given? Preferably once a week at the same time and same place. Consistency is important to establishing a pattern that children can count on. **Remember to honor your word by having their allowance ready each week on time.**

Can Allowances be Taken Away for Poor Behavior? Having read this far in the book you probably already know what the answer is. It is "No!" Taking money away for poor behavior is a form of punishment that creates bad feelings and resentment—not the qualities that support positive learning. Thus far, I have given you a potpourri of strategies that are effective for dealing with difficult behavior—use these instead.

Should an Allowance be Given for Good Marks in School? Probably of no surprise to you, again the answer is "No!" By all means celebrate— do a toast at dinner, go for a special outing or buy a round of ice cream! When it comes to your children's accomplishments the biggest benefit should be the satisfaction of knowing that their efforts paid off—a sense of feeling proud. **Personal pride (giving one's self a pat on the back) is what will motivate your children's future accomplishments.** When parents pay their children for grades in school they run the risk of acquiring big expenses if their children start demanding higher wages later on.

"Piggy Banking with a Twist": an Allowance System that Your Kids Will Love!

When it comes to allowances many children are given a piggy bank to hold their coin. Did you ever have one as a child? Kids often have some sort of "piggy bank" system whether shaped as a pig or not. What did yours look like? Was it one of those ceramic pigs that had to be broken in order to get the money out? Perhaps, you had a "piggy bank" with a little trap door on the bottom that ensured you had unlimited access? If this was the case, your savings may not have lasted long! Each type of piggy bank—the ceramic or trapped door kind—had a specific purpose. One enabled you to save and the other enabled you to spend. We want our kids to do both and more!

In order to start receiving an allowance your child simply has to agree to use the "piggy banking with a twist" system. Instead of having one piggy bank you want them to have four! These can be bought or made with jars and art scraps from around the house.

Your Child's Four Piggy Banks:

1. **"Super Savings Pig"**—This is your child's long-term savings. It can help him to learn the benefits of delayed gratification as he experiences his money accumulating over time. Eventually, you will want to deposit this money into his first savings account. Once the money goes into the bank, discuss with your child how interest works and show him how his money grows.

2. **"Play Dough Pig"**—This is your child's fun money. It is to be spent on a weekly basis for immediate gratification! Things like candy or a small trinket. This money is to be used to buy the things she wants without having to ask you for it. It also teaches her about what happens when she runs out of money. She can either find a way to make some money or simply wait for her next allowance.

3. **"Grand Goal Pig"**—Have your child choose an item that is just a bit out of his spending range. Help him to research the cost and to track down a picture of his desired purchase. Post a picture of his goal somewhere where he will regularly see it (on the jar is useful) and have him save up the required amount. In the beginning, choose an item that won't take any longer than a couple of months to save up for. Moms report that their child feels a deep sense of accomplishment and that he takes far better care of the toys that were bought with his money.

4. **"Kind Charity Pig"**—This one account helps instill the value of giving to others. Whether it goes to your religious organization, the animal shelter, or a children's hospital. Have your child choose a charity that excites her. When your child is ready to make her donation ensure that she is the one who mails or hand delivers it—not you.

The above accounts are the main building blocks that will begin to launch your children's money future. Most kids find it easiest to put 25% in each account. Older children may want to massage these percentages. **The rule of thumb for the "Super Savings Pig" and for the "Kind Charity Pig" is a minimum of 10%. This is the only rule that is a requirement of receiving an allowance.** As your kids get older they may want to create other accounts like: a "fun in the sun" holiday account or "best invest" account that they can use to start purchasing stocks or save up for a down payment on real estate property. You might be amazed at how quickly kids can become motivated by investing, saving, earning and spending.

The New Rules of Shopping with Your Kids

Shopping will never be the same once you implement allowances. Now when they ask, "Can I have that?" you simply ask, "Do you have enough money?" It is important to establish what you will pay for and what they will pay for early on. Discuss this at length. Even write it down in a simple "contract" being certain that you cover all areas like: dinners out, entertainment, and treats at the corner store. Many families make a deal that when they go out for dinner or to a movie together, Mom or dad pays for the basics but the kids pay for the extra treats (like pop and dessert). Treats at the store are almost always the children's responsibility. **Be clear on what you will pay for because children learn fast when you start making exceptions to the rule and will come to expect it.**

This brings up another question: what if you don't like what your kids have bought? Sometimes your children may want a cheap toy that you know will soon break or candy that you would rather they didn't have. The best thing to do is to allow them the experience without any interference from you. The natural consequence of having the toy break is a wonderful learning opportunity. When it comes to candy *[being a health buff, I do find this difficult!]* if we never allow them to have it, the more they will want junk food. **Allow your children to spend their "play dough" money as they wish. This is a form of respect and can teach your children how to spend wisely.**

Responsibilities that Set Your Child Up for Life

The more your child learns while they are under your roof, the more they will be prepared for life on their own. As your child masters the smaller steps, you can begin to give them more money responsibilities. Here is a list of money responsibilities for each stage of your child's development:

Toddlers and Money:

- Help them to pay for little purchases on their own. Practice this at home.
- Ask them to help you to count out or identify coins that you need when at a parking meter or when at the store.
- Help them to count out the money in their four "piggy bank with a twist" jars.
- Explain where money comes from when you are at ATM machines. Share with your children that you are taking money out that the bank is keeping for you and that if you spend all of it, nothing will be left until you put more in.

Children and Money:

- Have them learn about receiving correct change.
- Explain how credit cards and checks work.
- Ask them to help you estimate how much your groceries are going to be before you get to the check out line.
- Open their first savings account if you haven't already.
- Go through a list of the family expenses during a "family meeting."
- Take your kids on a tour of where you work (or where their dad works) and talk about where the money for the household comes from.

Tweens and Money:

- Accompany them to the bank to apply for their first ATM card and explain how it is used.
- Discuss or have someone else explain compound interest.

- At a "family meeting" have your tween help you pay the bills.
- Start reading books on money or investments as soon as they become interested in money.
- Go over how much you make, how much you pay in taxes, and how much your monthly expenses are.
- Give them the entire amount of money needed (in addition to their allowance) to buy their own school supplies. Have them make the purchase with little guidance from you.

Teens and Money:
- Take them to the bank to open their own checking account. Teach them how to use the ledger. If you aren't good at this ask a friend to teach both of you!
- Give them a quarterly clothing allowance. If they run out of money do not buy items for them (even if they need them). Kindly let them experience waiting for the following season.
- Go through your Will, education accounts, and any life insurance policies if you haven't already done so.
- Apply for a pre-paid credit card. This allows them to spend only what they have deposited on the low credit card. It also guides them to learn how to use credit wisely in addition to building their own credit.

When it comes down to it, nothing can teach your children more about managing money then getting them to manage their own money now.

Extra Money: How to Handle Part-Time Jobs and Your Kids

There may come a time when your child wants to earn some extra "play dough!" Support them. You can offer them tasks around the house that you would normally pay someone else to do. Things like: mowing the lawn, raking the leaves, gardening, washing the car, painting the house, or even basic filing. Come up with a fair rate and draw up a simple contract that covers all your expectations, a date for completion, and an agreed upon price. Sign the contract and make certain you both understand the terms of the agreement. Pay only upon completion.

Looking for a job outside the home can provide invaluable lessons especially during the summer months. Creating a resumé, going to an interview, and working for others are skill building opportunities. Paper routes, lifeguarding, babysitting, and anything else they can think of provide excellent experience. Find a way to help your children to balance school, work, and some play too! Also, have them look at acquiring skills that they are interested in by volunteering.

How to Create the Perfect Start to Your Kid's Financial Future

Teaching your kids about money can turn into a ritual that can actually bring you closer together. Special rituals are an important part of the human experience and are sometimes lost in our culture. As "Ultimate Moms," let's bring the magic back by incorporating a special allowance ritual. When you first start your child off with an allowance turn it into a rites of passage ritual by drawing up an allowance agreement. Have a gift (a purse or wallet) wrapped up for them to hold their "play dough." Explain the purpose of the allowance and ask them if they agree to the requirements. You may even want to create a small oath like the one below to really make it official. Kids love this! For younger children you can simplify it and have them repeat after you. For older kids you can write or type it out and have them read their part to you, as you read your part to them.

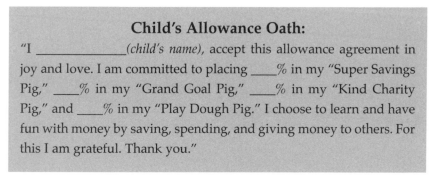

Child's Allowance Oath:

"I _____*(child's name)*, accept this allowance agreement in joy and love. I am committed to placing ____% in my "Super Savings Pig," ____% in my "Grand Goal Pig," ____% in my "Kind Charity Pig," and ____% in my "Play Dough Pig." I choose to learn and have fun with money by saving, spending, and giving money to others. For this I am grateful. Thank you."

> ## Mom's Allowance Oath:
>
> "I _____(*your name*), accept this allowance agreement in joy and love. I am committed to supporting _____(*child's name*) by giving them $____ every week on _____(*day*) at _____ (*time*). I choose to learn and have fun with money by being committed to earning, saving, spending, and investing and by supporting my child to learn about how to mange money in a healthy way. I love _____(*child's name*) and am grateful for this opportunity to support _____(*child's name*) in becoming an amazing money manager. Thank you."

After the allowance ceremony take time to celebrate this new beginning together *[tickling fight anyone?]!*

Chapter Tips:

1. Your children are learning every day about money by your very actions. Therefore, you are the *best* person to teach them about finances. Allow this to inspire you to improve!

2. An allowance is the most effective way to teach your children about money. It gives them the opportunity to make mistakes now that can result in future financial wisdom as adults.

3. "Piggy banking with a twist" gives your children the greatest opportunity to learn how to save, spend and give to charity.

Taking Action:

1. At your next "family meeting" have an allowance ceremony and find a way to make it special for your children.

2. In the next week, make a conscious effort to explain how "plastic" works to your children.

3. Choose to get your own finances in order by learning how to pay yourself first, reduce your debt and spend wisely. **If you would like some assistance in this area download (for free) my special report called, "Discover the Treasure that Lies in Your Family Pay Check" that covers each of these areas by going to www.ultimateparenting.com/bookdownloads.**

Dear Diary,

"Writers block" is what some would say I have. More than "writers block," I think I have "scaredy cat" block. Why would people listen to me talk about God in the final chapter of the book? How can I write about something that is so much of a "feeling" for me? Why me? Why not me? If not me, who?

I have been to synagogues in Old Jerusalem, the Nativity Church in Bethlehem, Buddhist Temples in Thailand, Sikh Temples in India, and stood in the Pyramids of Giza. Yet, where I experience my spiritual connection most, is in the early mornings of silence, in the eyes of a curious child, and in the sighting of a deer in the woods. I don't just experience "God" on Sunday; I strive to connect with the light within me every day. Granted I fall short many times, but sometimes I feel spirit move me in ways I once thought impossible.

When it comes to God, I am not a preacher, a rabbi, nor a minister; I am simply a woman seeking to leave the world better than I found it. I want to experience my relationship with God minute after minute, and to get through the ups and downs with faith, strength and gratitude. Everyone's connection to the divine is different. Mine is just as important as everyone else's and this is why I have the authority to write as I am now. Kelly, just be honest, write from your heart and have the courage to continue to bare your soul.

Kelly

IS YOUR G-SPOT A BIG PART OF YOUR LIFE?

Why Your G-Spot is So Important

Gotcha! With a title like this I know many of you were so curious you might have chosen to start the book right here! No matter how you found yourself at this page, I do know one thing about you: you are a Mom who longs to bring out the very best in your children. One of the easiest ways to do this is by bringing God into your life. Whether you call it—God, Buddha, Light, Allah, Divinity, or Love—when you invite "it" into your day-to-day activities you can begin to experience untold blessings, and yes, passion too!

Finding God for me was kind of like finding the elusive and mysterious "G-spot" that many sex educators refer to. I knew it was there, but how in the world do you access it when you can't feel nor see it? And how the heck do you find "it" when you need "it" most? Can you relate? Do you ever experience those "blah days," "blah weeks," and even "blah months?" Have you ever lost that "loving feeling," wish your "snooze button" could go on forever, and wish you could curl up like a bear under your covers and hibernate for the winter? It's during these times that you need to call on something larger than yourself. Doing so can provide comfort, guidance, and faith that in the end it's all going to work out—and somehow it always does.

Our connection to the divine acts as our compass in the stormy weather of life. God guides us to safety and is our "true north star" that protects us with it's light. Having the belief that there is something larger than ourselves gives us the strength to make the changes we know we need to make. Tapping into your spiritual "G-spot," the God-spot—that place where spirit becomes a part of your daily life, is an essential part to getting through those challenging "deep end" moments. It also guides you to be able to make life decisions that are in keeping with what's in your heart. I write this chapter to illuminate, to encourage and to inspire you to access your spiritual life. Whatever your belief in God, I trust that you will change the wording of this chapter in order to find something that works best for you. You will know what is best—just listen and you will know.

Could Lack of Spirit be the Missing Link You Seek?

God or no God, have you ever done everything right to only have it feel completely wrong? You may be going through all the right motions, saying all the right things and still feel as though something is missing. You are being the best Mom, the best friend, the best lover, and the best you that you can be and yet, something just doesn't feel right. It might be that empty pit in your stomach or that lack of purpose that you feel in your life. If this is the case, the missing link might just be a lack of spirit in your life and in your family's life.

What is this "spirit" that I speak of? It is the invisible essence that makes us human; where love and miracles are felt and experienced. The moments when peace falls over you, where joy pulses through you, and when you love so totally you have no fear of rejection. It is the state that all religions speak of. It is that belief in something larger than oneself. **"Spirit" is a deep knowing that you are here for a purpose and that your life is a statement of that purpose.** It gives us the strength to see past our mistakes and other's mistakes. It also gives us the courage to let go of our fears and love more deeply. **Spirit leads us to realize that the only true risk in life is not expressing who we really are, and not sharing our light with our family and loved ones.**

How do You Access Spirit?

Is it realistic to think that we can really maintain this kind of state? If we did it might feel as though we were "in love" a lot of the time! Imagine, feeling like you were madly head over heels in love every single day! Kind of nice wouldn't you say? So how do we achieve this state, and then maintain it?

When I feel at a loss, you will find me saying a prayer while in a bubble bath, on the phone with a girlfriend, cuddled up next to my sweetie, or alone in nature. Nothing can dry my tears and dissolve my problems like the wind off the ocean; returning me cleansed in mind, in body and in spirit. I sometimes sit, I cry, I seek, and I find the answer that was there all along. What is it that brings you real comfort?

Throughout my life (and in my work with clients) I have witnessed the most profound transformations and miracles when people tap into spirit, especially during the times they literally want to jump off the "deep end!" **I am convinced that you and I are as powerful and sparkling as the North Star yet, small and insignificant when viewed within the entire solar system.** We touch our greatness when we start to work with "spirit" to create the life of our dreams. In the next section, you will find practical ways that my clients and I have used to bring more spirit into our lives. By choosing to do so, little by little, you can experience greater comfort that helps you through those "bad hair" moments.

Twenty Ways to Invite More Spirit into Your Family Life:

1. Wake up each morning and ask yourself, "What is the one thing that I will do today that will really make a difference?"
2. Join a supportive social or religious group that meets on a regular basis. Make certain that the values and people within the group are people that you *want* to spend time with.
3. Regularly read over your "Wish Upon a Star 100 List" *[Chapter Three]*.
4. Start doing the "Thank You Fors" exercise described at the end of this chapter.

5. Greet each of your family members at least once a day with statements like, "I am so blessed to have you in my life!" "You are gorgeous!" "I am the luckiest Mom in the world to have a child as wonderful as you in my life!"

6. Spend at least five minutes each day in silence.

7. Read inspirational material at least once a day.

8. Cut back on the amount that you read the paper and spend less time watching the evening news.

9. Spend at least once a week in your garden, on a long walk, or in a park.

10. Take time to dream and follow your own passions [see Chapter Three for more!].

11. Each month do something you have never done before, or go to a place you have always wanted to go.

12. Focus on what you are grateful for in your life—more and more each and every day.

13. Learn how to breathe deeply and do it on a regular basis.

14. Stretch and exercise regularly.

15. When you look at people smile with your eyes.

16. Choose to never go to bed mad. Instead clear the air and choose to forgive each person in your life daily.

17. Watch more funny movies.

18. Have more tickle fights!

19. Tell more jokes.

20. Treat everyone like they are the greatest miracle in the world including you!

How You Can Experience Miracles

When you choose an abundant approach to life you are choosing to believe and invite miracles into your life. This means knowing that you deserve all the love, support, nurturing, pampering, vitality, passion, encouragement, confidence, peace, and trust that you can imagine. **Miracles occur when you believe that they will and when you know in your heart that you deserve them.** I am here to tell you in this moment, through this page that you are holding (or on the screen that you are reading), that no matter where you are or where you have come from—you deserve miracles! When we buy into our insecurities and our fears we start living a lie. **Who you truly are is a magnificent woman—no less and no more than all the other amazing women out there! Your kids deserve a truly magnificent woman to be their Mom. This Mom is you!** Believing anything less is living a lie that only keeps your light hidden.

How do we foster an abundant approach to life? By learning to listen to our heart (also called intuition), by loving ourselves, by sharing our love, by being honest with our fears, and by standing up for what we believe in. When we start doing all these things we have the courage to create our best life for ourselves *[reread Chapter Three for more]* and for our family. **Inviting miracles into your life happens when you expect the best and see the glass of life as forever half full—full enough to provide all our needs and empty enough to leave space for the magic to occur.**

Divine spirit enters our lives when we act as if our life totally depended upon our own actions, but we surrender to the outcome as if everything depended upon God. Sometimes this requires that we "act as if" and go with the flow. It means enjoying the process of life and not getting hung up on the outcome especially when it doesn't look so rosy. **It is important to remember that in an abundant world what appears to be a failure or setback is just a different path that will lead us to something even greater.** Trust this. Believe this.

Are You Choosing to be an Optimist?

When life gives you manure get digging! The following story exemplifies the power of a true optimist who makes lemonade out of the lemons in life:

> There once was a family that had twin boys whose only resemblance to each other were their looks. If one felt it was too hot, the other thought it was too cold. If one said the TV was too loud, the other claimed the volume needed to be turned up. Opposite in every way, one was an eternal optimist, the other a doom and gloom pessimist.

Out of curiosity, on the twins' birthday their father loaded the pessimist's room with every imaginable toy and game and the optimist's room he loaded with horse manure. That night the father passed by the pessimist's room and found him sitting amid his new gifts crying bitterly. "Why are you crying?" the father asked. "Because I'll have to read all these instructions before I can do anything with these toys that will eventually break anyhow." the pessimist twin answered. Passing the optimist's room, the father found him dancing for joy in the pile of manure. "What are you so happy about?" he asked. To which his optimist twin replied, "There's got to be a pony in here somewhere!"

Which sibling are you? Are you choosing to be the half-full optimist or the half-empty pessimist? Choosing to be an optimist means ensuring that you are making the most out of what you've got. Your inspiration—that sparkle that burns from the inside out is the key to making the most of the life you have been given. It allows you to naturally assists others, especially your kids, in bringing out their very best too.

How to Shrink Your Problems to a Manageable Size

When you reach the rough patches in life and are up to your knees in manure, there is nothing like "spirit" to provide the comfort, faith, and strength to get you through. This connection can instantly give you perspective—namely that your troubles are often far more manageable than they at first appear. When you are in touch with your own "spirit", you suddenly discover options and solutions that you may have never thought possible. With "spirit's" help you can also access the grace that empowers you to work through and let go of the beliefs [and sometimes even people!] that keep you stuck in the yuck! **Your relationship to God can help you realize that in the grand scheme of things, your problems are a mere freckle on your life's face.** Your connection (when activated) allows you to get back into touch with the life that you were meant to live. If you are struggling with what you want to do, who you want to be, or wondering what your purpose is, your heart is the place to start.

Shrinking Your Problems and Accessing Your Heart Requires You to do the Following:

1. Choose to look for options and brainstorm solutions.
2. Break down problems into bite-size steps and work on one step at a time.
3. Ask for help and accept it when it comes.
4. Be willing to take action and change what is not working.
5. Take responsibility for that which you can change and gracefully accept that which you can't.

It is also essential that you catapult yourself out of any self-pitying experiences that are keeping you stuck. This requires taking action, reaching out, and having faith that your current situation will change.

How to Eliminate Self-Pity and Let Your Light Shine:

1. Realize that things aren't what they first seem. An apparent setback can be a gift in disguise.
2. Repeat to yourself over and over, "This too shall pass!"
3. Do something to make someone else smile.
4. Focus only on what you can change and do it!
5. Pray for guidance and expect it to come.
6. Use a pattern-interrupt—go for a walk, take a "Mom's Time-Out," breathe deep, work in a garden, or take in a "fluffy chick-flick!"

Taking some time for yourself to be with "spirit" is what will reconnect you to your heart. Sometimes this connection will be as simple as taking a bath, reading a chapter in a fantasy novel or a passage from your favorite spiritual text, taking ten deep breaths or going on a weekend away from everything by yourself! **"No, but I couldn't go away for an entire weekend!" you might say. If more mothers would go on weekends away and actually respond to their own warning signals, I believe we would have far less Moms on anti-depressants, desperately wanting to numb their pain.** One client wrote me recently saying: "I took a weekend off just last week—it was the most liberating experience! When I returned I was like a new Mom and you know what? My kids and husband needed the break too. Kelly thanks for making it OK for me to nurture myself. I now feel like I am on my second honeymoon!"

How to Renew Your Innocence and Sense of Play

Reconnecting with ourselves means renewing our sense of fun and play! The Lord's Prayer adorned my wall as a child and I would repeat it before going to sleep full of peace. There was also a special tree that I planted outside in my front yard that I would speak to on a regular basis. Yes, I spoke to trees! Did any of you? I spoke to my tree as if it were full of fairies that could hear my inner most thoughts, concerns, and dreams. And then my parents got divorced, we moved, and the magic seemed to fade away. I got older, more busied, more stressed and more serious! I let my "inner child" go. It wasn't until I had chronic fatigue that I really began to allow my "inner child" to come back out and play. I don't know about you, but when I am playful, when I give myself permission to be wacky, I feel closer to my heart and soul. In these moments, I am also able to give love more freely.

When is the last time that you really had fun, when you laughed from deep down in your belly, when a true smile broke out over your face, and that sparkle in your eye shone through? We all have these moments. Few for some, but we can all access them. The things that made us smile as a child often still make us smile as a Mom today—swinging on the swings, dressing up, putting on nail polish, swimming in the lake naked, tobogganing, playing hide and go seek, or looking for special shells on the beach.

I have a couple of girlfriends that are willing to do crazy things with me. We crazy carpet down mountains in the winter, giggle together at what we call "spa nights," skinny dip in the summer and laugh over old boyfriend stories on walks. Most recently we have been planning an evening in wedding dresses—girls only! Outrageous? Yes! **Do you have those silly thoughts? Those "What if I had the guts to do..." thoughts? Make a plan to start doing some of them and recapture the little girl within you who has been dying to come out and play.**

Your G-Spot

Before I continue, allow me to clear up a common misunderstanding between "child-like" and "childish." Playing full on with a skip in your step and joy in your heart is tapping into the "child-like" aspect of your being. This promotes good health and a happy life. Being "childish" is not just reserved for children. Childishness is what is demonstrated in the millions of adults who are depressed. **Depression in Moms is simply their "inner child" having a silent tempter tantrum begging to be set free. Curing unhappiness and depression lies in giving ourselves permission to do, to be, and to have what we know in our hearts we deserve.**

How to Include Gratitude on a Daily Basis

But who has the time to play? Many Moms are trapped by the confines of a hectic life. So much to do—so little time. Yet, what if the items on our "to-do" gave us more life, more energy, and more enthusiasm? Wouldn't this list be worth your time? Gratitude, like play, is an item that feeds your soul. **The key to gratitude is simple. It is focusing on what you have, rather than on what you don't have.**

Gratitude can become a part of your family's life in terms of saying grace or using family rituals *[suggested in Chapter Five]*. These can be conventional or totally unconventional—your choice. Have you ever sat down *[finally!]* at the dinner table only to be depressed by the conversation that includes bickering, nit picking, and negative discussion? Add this to the six o'clock news and you may want to call it a day!

Four years ago, this is exactly what was happening at the dinner table. Grant and Graham would squabble over pretty much everything! Out of pure desperation I had a sudden insight. I called it "Thank You Fors" and made it into a game. Each of us would take a turn and share what we were thankful for. The first week things didn't go well, especially when I heard comments from Graham like, "I am thankful that my brother didn't bug me as much as he usually does." But slowly it became a spiritual tradition that they have come to expect and enjoy. One night I sat with tears in my eyes as Graham said, "I am thankful for my brother's success today." There was a time when I wondered if they would ever be able to show appreciation for one another.

Gratitude doesn't have to be in the form of a regular ritual to be effective. It can happen "on the run." Place a sticky note in your car with the word "gratitude" written on it. Every time you get in the car think about one thing that you are grateful for. By choosing to do this, you are building a life giving habit. **Using gratitude regularly is like putting gasoline into the car of your life—it helps you to move, to accelerate, and to travel to where you want to go.** When you focus on what you do have and take the time to appreciate your life, you will naturally attract more in your life that you are grateful for. **Gratitude is not about paying "lip service"—it is a sincere thank you from your heart to God's.**

How We Know it Will All Work Out in the End

Life isn't easy—it's worth it, it's marvelous, it's magical—but it isn't easy. To believe it will all work out in the end can be tough, especially when we get caught up in the chaos of our lives. When you are right in the "deep end" it can sometimes appear that the feelings of upset and hurt will never go away. But they always do. Life is forever changing—this is the only thing we can be certain of.

Often, it is the most difficult challenges in life that force us out of our comfort zone. These challenges can lead us to greater successes, deeper relationships, and increased joy. In grade twelve, I was convinced that my current boyfriend would one day become my husband. To hear otherwise made me only want it more. Yet, he had other plans *[namely another girl who caught his eye]*. When I found out, I thought I'd just die! Yet, now in my 30's, I am so thankful that he *was* attracted to her and got caught up in the moment!

If I were to ask you what was one of the most difficult experiences of your life would you have an answer? Do you have an experience that changed over time? Where your feelings changed? Perhaps, you even feel it was now somehow a gift—a blessing. When you are smack dab in the "deep end" it is helpful to keep your faith and to remember, "that this too shall pass." I promise!

Choose to live your life by looking for the silver lining in every cloud. Even when you are in the midst of a storm, the glowing sun is often only moments away! **And while you are waiting for the clouds to pass, remind yourself to, "Let go, and let God."** If you can't change it, surrender it, and trust that the challenge will be taken care of in due time. "Let go and let God" is the motto for this chapter—it may become your personal motto. Is there anything you want to let go of "Ultimate Mom?" God is waiting.

Chapter Tips:

1. Believing in something greater than yourself can give you the strength to start living your best life.
2. You are truly a magnificent woman! Your kids deserve a truly magnificent woman to be their Mom by having you shine brightly!
3. Living life with gratitude is a gift to both you and your family. It has the power to transform your life—giving you even greater blessings.

Taking Action:

1. When dealing with difficult situations one of my mentors, Minister Mary Manin Morrisey, suggests asking, "What would love do in this situation?" Commit to asking this.
2. When is the last time you filled up your own spiritual cup? Choose one thing and commit to doing it within the next week.
3. Start your own gratitude journal and encourage your children to do the same. Write down what you are thankful for and share it with your family.

YOU ARE AN "ULTIMATE MOM!"

Before we begin this last chapter, I want to deeply thank you for your commitment to reading this book. By doing so, you have proven by your very actions that you are already starting to access the "Ultimate Mom" within you. It is Moms just like you who inspire me to do what I do!

Sitting here writing the conclusion to the book I ask myself: why have I just shared all of these thoughts and tools with you? Why have I spent thousands of hours pouring over this book *[which is now over 63, 410 words!]*? Why have I put off *so* many other priorities to complete this one? The answer is clear. **My mission is to share "Mom-ming" strategies that help to create a world in which our children grow up knowing how truly amazing they are—a world in which mothers are supported in bringing out the best in themselves and in their children.** I believe in a world where children are guided to discover their passions and inspired to dedicate their gifts to the betterment of humanity. We need more of this in the world. We need this right now. Every time I watch the evening news I become more convinced of the fact that changes are needed. **It isn't about more jails, more laws, or more punishment— it *is* about using a new approach. The "Ultimate Mom" approach can be implemented by Moms just like you! This approach heals our communities by first healing our homes.**

Allow me to share one last story with you:

> There once were two monks that came across a river. Their meditative state was suddenly broken by dozens of cries from children that were drowning in the river. The first monk jumped in (clothes and all) attempting to save each one. But there were just too many. The second monk disappeared. Hours later the first monk exhausted sat on the shore feeling badly that he hadn't saved more children. The second returned. "Where did you go?" the first asked angrily. The second replied, "Upstream to find and stop the person who was throwing them in."

Rather than focusing all our energy on rescuing the hoard of angry, depressed and irresponsible young adults, it is time to head upstream. Each of us has within us the tools that can support and nurture our children to lead the next generation toward greatness! We can lead our children toward a life of compassion and of contribution. **It is time that prevention started in our homes. From the "Ultimate Mom" in each of you, I believe we can create an "Ultimate Planet"—of this I am certain.**

Join "The 1,000,000 Ultimate Mom Challenge!"

I have a dream and it is a very big dream. It could possibly involve you! You see, alone, I *can* make a difference. With you, *we can make a tremendous difference.* I want the "Ultimate Mom" program to inspire at least 1,000,000 regular Moms to become 1,000,000 "Ultimate Moms." Why? Our future depends upon the generation that we are raising now. The future of our children requires us to step up and empower them by empowering ourselves. **Help the next generation by passing this book on.**

From the bottom of my heart I believe we can make a significant difference by spreading the "Ultimate Mom" approach. The more Moms that are using this material, the less future young adults will be seeking solutions in crime, in depression and in drugs and alcohol. **If you feel inspired to continue to work towards being the best**

Mom you can be, I invite you to join our "1,000,000 Ultimate Mom Challenge" at www.ultimateparenting.com and receive your FREE "Mommy Moments." These daily email reminders can make a world of difference.

A million Moms declaring that they are "Ultimate Moms" is my goal. Imagine what a world we would live in if millions of Moms let their own brilliance shine and inspired their children to do the same? This is the world I dream of and for the sake of our future, our children's future, and our planets future we need to act now. It is time that we did, what we know in our hearts to be true.

Will You Accept this Job?

WANTED

1,000,000 "Ultimate Moms" for a position of a lifetime
that can't help but bring out the best in you!

NO SALARY, BUT UNLIMITED BENEFITS!

Seeking "Ultimate Moms" who are willing to become more than what they may have once thought possible. Responsible for being honest, doing your best and taking care of yourself so you can take care of the kids! Ability to take "Mom Time-Outs," to encourage your children in their passions (while accessing your own) and the ability to look for the good in others are all great assets to this position. Courage to risk and to make mistakes required! "Super Moms" need not apply but recovering "Super Moms" are welcome!

NO PAY
(but you will receive unexpected benefits beyond your wildest dreams!)

NO DENTAL COVERAGE
(but you are given the opportunity to smile and laugh on a regular basis!)

NO MEDICAL COVERAGE
(but an unlimited supply of love!)

Job, heart and soul security guaranteed.

*NOTE: APPLICATION TAKES ONLY A MOMENT OF GETTING IN TOUCH WITH YOUR OWN HEART.

To apply contact: www.ultimateparenting.com.

keep in touch with the "Ultimate Mom" in you

Dear "Ultimate Mom," (yes, I do mean you! ☺)

If someone hasn't told you lately … **You are AWESOME and deserve all that life has to offer!** *I hope to continue to play a part in your life by having you join us at* **www.ultimateparenting.com.**

Please visit our website www.ultimateparenting.com to review:
- How You can Receive Your "Mommy Moments" Free.
- Our Additional "Mom-ming Products and Information."
- How you can join the "1,000,000 Ultimate Mom Challenge."
- Ultimate Parenting Events and My Appearances and Interviews.
- Frequently Asked Questions (FAQ's) About Our Products and Information.
- Kelly's CD titled: *How to Raise Fabulous Kids in 10 Minutes a Day: for Mom's With Little to No Time.*

Unleashing the "Ultimate Mom" in you is a daily choice—a daily decision. Our websites and products are designed to support you on each step of your journey that will inspire you and your family to live your best life ever!

Fondly, with hugs and blessings,

Index

C

N

O

P

U

V

W

Y

ultimate mom"
notes...

ultimate mom" notes...

ultimate mom" notes...

dream healer & con

chore wheel a chore jar
family muting agnda

created especially for you...

To order books or CDs for your organization or group, or simply to give as gifts to your deserving friends visit:
www.ultimateparenting.com
or call toll free: **1-888-233-5652**

Please have the following information ready:

Last Name _____ First Name _____

Address _____

City _____ State/Province _____

Zip/Postal Code _____ Country _____

Phone Number _____ Email Address _____

Credit Card # _____ Expiry Date _____

now available:

- Book $19.95US / $26.95CDN: *When You're About to go off the Deep End, Don't Take Your Kids with You*

- CD $19.95US / $26.95CDN: *How to Raise Fabulous Kids in 10 Minutes a Day: for Mom's with Little or No Time*

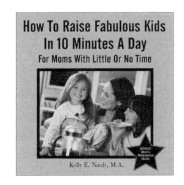

kelly

by Grant Hardy

Kelly, you have an inspiring mind,
You're always sweet and you're always kind.
You have many passions,
And many generous dreams,
You have many kind hopes,
You have kindness to it's extremes.
You have many loving visions,
And creative and wonderful plans,
You have many thoughtful missions,
Every day your love expands.

You take refreshing long walks,
Across the land of Peace and Good Times,
Swim across the rivers of abundance,
Like the glowing light the sun shines.

You open the doors to giving,
You extend the halls of forgiving,
You live the moments of gentleness,
You know how life's worth living.

You're like the water in the sea of fulfillment,
You're like the sun in the skies where love's made,
You're like the nests in the trees where kindness grows,
You're like the grass where peace laid.

You're like the sun shining down from the sky,
You're like the sun shining high.
You're like the whispering calming sound of the wind at night,
You're like the shining passion and dreams light.

— *Written for Kelly's birthday in 2002*
BY GRANT HARDY, then age 12

about the author
kelly e. nault

Kelly Nault, M.A., is the President and CEO of Ultimate Parenting, a business dedicated to setting achievable standards of excellence for motherhood. Kelly offers Moms a rare combination of cutting-edge—and above all—easy "Mom-ming" tools. As a parenting expert, Kelly reminds Moms (and yes, sometimes dads too!) of how important and valuable their role is, while providing an assortment of strategies that take the stressful guesswork out of the parenting equation. A gifted presenter who speaks from the heart, Kelly inspires her audiences to not just "let" motherhood happen, but to "learn" how to make motherhood an enriching and enjoyable experience for both Mom and child. As a pioneer of "Mothering in the 21st Century," Kelly believes that supporting Moms to reach their highest fulfillment in life is necessary for raising a generation of happy, responsible and compassionate children. She created the CD, *How to Raise Fabulous Kids in 10 Minutes A Day: for Moms With Little or No Time* and lives in Vancouver, British Columbia. To learn more about Kelly and Ultimate Parenting visit **www.ultimateparenting.com**

magnet board - magnets

- bingo chips at end
     of day

- end of week bingo
chips turned in for
predetermined reward.

	Luke	Tris	Josh
BACK PACKS			
PIANO			
ROOM			
Recycly vacum laundry			

• 3 diff. magnets shapes